**Dedicated to:
My Dad**

Chapters

Prologue
1/ The End
2/ Promotion Day
3/ The Service
4/ Super Bowl Sunday
5/ You Don't Understand
before
6/ Soulmates
7/ Margret
8/ Lies Before Kindergarten
9/ Sugar
10/ Wake Up
11/ Bath Time
12/ The BQE
13/ The Most Perfect Evening
14/ Manhole
15/ New School
16/ Christmas Pageant
17/ Ski Vacation
18/ What's Going On
19/ Bastards
20/ Blue Whistle Pops
21/ Secret
22/ Three One

23/ Don't Ever Come Back
24/ My Mom's Friends
25/ Public School
26/ Roland
27/ Hello
28/ Hindsight
after
29/ I Wasn't Ready
30/ Family Cruise
31/ South Korea
32/ Chartered School
33/ The Rock
34/ Goodbye Taekwondo
35/ Take Me Out to the Ballgame
36/ Detective Work
37/ 9/11
38/ My Dream Come True
39/ Incredible Luck
40/ Cheerleading
41/ You Can't Sit With Us
42/ My Only Friend
43/ Lunch Money
44/ I Know What I Saw
45/ It's Cold
46/ Hospital
47/ That's How the Night Goes
Epilogue

Prologue

I'm a thirty-year-old adult, and in one week I am going to turn thirty-one. I've spent the better part of my life feeling defective, broken, and alone. I've been a stripper for six years, and about three years ago I started doing stand-up comedy. I've been successful at both. As a stripper I make at least $1,000 a night. As a stand-up comedian I've made tremendous progress in the industry in an extremely short amount of time; possibly more than anyone else has ever made.

People think I'm cool now… like, really, really cool. Sometimes they think I'm famous. But I'm not. I'm still eleven years old, standing over my father's dead body. I'm still trying to figure out how it all went so wrong. I'm still dirty, hungry, injured, and diseased. I don't know how to make that go away. But I do know how to fake it. I know how to put on a good show. I know how to smile when everyone cheers. But I'm awkward every single time after the show when they come up to talk to me. I don't know how to make that go away.

The other big problem, for me, is podcasts. I'm on a lot of them, all the time. People always ask me about my story. I don't know what kind of nice life they had, but every time they ask, I tell them the truth, and they cringe. I don't like that. Why do people ask if they don't want to know the truth?

I wrote this book, I suppose, to reach others who are in need. I wrote it knowing that the things I've said will be taken out of context. I'll probably be strung up on a cross after this gets published. But maybe there's some kid out there whose parent just committed suicide, or who's on their third day with no food, or who's recovering in a hospital bed after being raped. Maybe that kid will check my book out of the library and learn the most important lesson I ever learned. I think if this reaches one kid, it'll be worth the potential ridicule, rejection, and damage to my career that this book might do.

In 1993 my hometown became the first municipality in the United States to disband its police department and hire a couple of private security guards instead.

I was only five years old at the time, so I

don't remember it, but I grew up hearing stories that the police were doing drug busts at people's houses, then they took the drugs and sold them out of the police station. The mayor made the decision to disband the police department.

Not having a police force led to a very chaotic town where a lot of criminals were able to exist without fear of police. There are some chapters in my book which, in a normal town, would have ended with the police showing up, but we had no police to call.

Some names and identifying details have been changed to protect the privacy of individuals.

1

The End

"Mom! Dad's not breathing!" Charley, my ten year old brother, blared.

I was asleep. I was warm. I was home. I was safe.

My head felt heavy on the pillow. Groggy, and barely opening my eyes, I could see a thick white blanket of snow covered the ground outside. I could hear my brother, already awake and getting ready for school, which meant I wasn't lucky enough for a snow day. Instead, I was dreading a math test. *Why, oh, why does sixth grade math have to be so difficult? But maybe*, I thought, *I'll be able to fake sick. What should my excuse be?*

My brother's words were emotionless, panic-free, deafening. They smacked onto the living room floor, catapulted down the hallway, crashed onto my bed. To anyone else, the words would have stung their soul. To me, they were an impossible, inconceivable mistake. They were the words of someone else's life. I was angry. Dad probably fell asleep on the couch. He probably didn't get called in for work that day because of the snowstorm, and now my stupid brother was going to make him wake up for no reason. Worse than that, my brother's idiotic stunt was messing up my plan of faking sick.

"Oh, my God," my mother shrieked. "Charles, please wake up!"

Not a mistake. Adrenaline surged through me. In one swift motion I threw my quilt toward the wall and swung my feet off my queen-sized bed. I hustled down the hallway, barely noticing how cold the wooden floor was. I turned the corner and stood in the arch of the living room. My initial thought was one of exasperated anxiety-induced humor: *I guess I won't be going to school today.*

My dad's favorite ratty old maroon robe was wrapped around him, but not keeping him warm, because there was nothing left to keep warm. In my eleven-year-old life, I'd never seen anything lay so still.

I passed the coffee table, which was covered in empty liquor bottles, a carton of ice cream, plates of cheesecake, and syringes. Sunken into the floral sofa, his body lay lifeless. He was blue, still, and cold. With no tears or understanding of the gravity of the situation, I laid my head on his chest, gripped him tightly, and closed my eyes. I breathed in the liquor, the cigarette smoke, and his after-shave.

A few nights before, I sat on his lap in the very same spot he was lying now. We played a game where he would squeeze his eyes shut and I would try to use my little fingers to pry them open. I thought to myself, *Okay, Daddy, let's see if I can win this time!* Effortlessly, I opened his eyelid; a single tear tumbled down his cheek. I stared at it because it didn't look like any tear I had ever seen. My daddy's dark brown eye, with its single tear, stared past me. It was empty and bleak. There was nothing there at all.

Without warning the coffee table plummeted down the opening to the spiral staircase my dad built before I was born. I whipped around to see my mother heaving for air. She was hysterical and my brother was obviously petrified. In my mind, I saw my health teacher's face, and I realized I had to go in the kitchen and get the phone.

"9-1-1, please state your emergency," the operator said.

Her calm tone and lethargic demeanor infuriated me.

"My dad's not breathing! He's dead!"

"Is your mother there with you?"

I passed my mother the phone.

I stood and watched her heave incoherently into the receiver, not even holding the ear piece next to her face. My mother passed the phone back to me.

"Okay, honey, I need you to be a big girl," said the operator.

I couldn't understand why she was talking to me as if I were a toddler.

"How old are you?" she asked.

"Eleven. Why?"

"What's your address?"

I told her. I was becoming angrier. Nothing she was saying was bringing my dad back to life.

"Do you know how old your dad is?"

Thank goodness, something I knew. "He's 42."

"Do you know if your dad has any medical problems?"

"I think he has diabetes, and there's something wrong with his back," I said.

The questions dragged on forever. At some point my mother reposed enough to take the phone from me. She told me to go in her bedroom to call her friend, Sophie. I left the living room for the sanctuary of my parents' bedroom, away from the chaos. I sat on their bed and dialed the second line. Sophie didn't answer her phone. I redialed, this time praying. Still no answer.

I went back to the living room to tell my mother. My brother was coming into the house with Mindy, our next-door neighbor, behind him. Pinning the phone between her ear and her shoulder, I watched as my mother and Mindy pulled my dad's massive, limp body off the couch, and on to the area rug. I peered over the railing to see the coffee table wedged between the wall and center support pole of the spiral stairs. Our white German Shepherd was trapped in the basement, barking, trying to fight her way up the stairs, past the broken glass and debris from the coffee table.

I retreated again to my parents' bedroom and sat on the bed. For the first time that morning, I started to cry. I sobbed uncontrollably.

Not knowing what else to do, I called my best friend, Emma. Into the phone I wailed, "My dad is dead, my dad is dead!" over and over and over, and I didn't understand why she couldn't hear me. The tears burned and I was choking, but she had to know.

"I have to go to school now," she said over my howling and hung up. I was stunned that this wasn't as devastating to her as it was to me. I stared at the sound of the dead phone line. I couldn't believe she just hung up like that. My brain couldn't comprehend the sound of a dead phone line was not something I could see. I sat there, holding the phone, looking at the sound, trying to understand what just happened.

Mindy's husband was pushing my brother and me out the front door. We were supposed to go to their house and wait for my mother. The last time I saw my dad's body, he was sprawled out on the living room area rug. My mother and Mindy were frantically trying to perform CPR. I thought, *That's not what I remember CPR looking like in health class.*

At Mindy's house their daughters, who were a year and two years older than me, were leaving for school. Their younger brother was in the den playing video games. He didn't have to go to kindergarten until later that day.

"Why aren't you guys going to the bus stop?" Kimberly, their middle daughter who was a grade ahead of me, asked.

I didn't answer her. Her father pushed her and her sister out the door. I looked after them as they left tracks in the deep snow and walked down the hill. At the bottom of the hill, other students waiting at the bus stop gawked at the ambulances lined up on the street in front of my house.

"Go play video games with Jimmy," I told Charley. I let the weight of our tragedy culminate in my mind. I realized Jimmy was too young to understand this disaster, and it would not be beneficial for him to know what was happening. "But don't tell him why we're here."

I sat in the family room and calmly wrote a letter to Grand Master Kwan, my martial arts instructor. My father died on a Thursday. Together, we were supposed to test for our black belts on Saturday. I wrote that my father had worked incredibly hard to achieve his black belt. My black belt no longer mattered to me and I wanted nothing more than to do the promotion test in my father's honor and earn his belt. As I sat writing the letter, a steady stream of tears fell from my eyes. They left big round stains on the paper, which made the ink smear. I felt collected, not erratic. Solemn and steady, not depressed or frantic.

Finally, I heard the front door open. Entering the living room, my brother and I saw our distraught, disheveled mother, hollow and exhausted. Behind her stood Grand Master Kwan and Sophie. My mother was able to get in contact with them, regarding the news of my dad. Despite the icy road conditions they both hurried over. Together with our neighbors, our family friends watched as our mother fell to her knees. My brother and I ran into her arms.

"God wanted Daddy to come home," my mother said. "The angels came and took him to heaven."

Together my shattered family wept. For a long time, I stayed in my mother's arms, not caring that onlookers were watching the earth crumble beneath us. Though I knew before she told us, the confirmation that my father really was gone was suffocating me. I felt I could faint at any second.

I wanted to stay with her desperately, but my mother said we had to go over Grand Master Kwan's house and wait until she was ready to get us. I pleaded to stay with her. She explained that she had to go to the hospital and call my sister and the rest of our family. I felt discarded and useless.

Obediently, my brother pulled on his winter coat and boots. I went into the family room and retrieved the letter I had been writing. I folded it in half, then in half again. When I returned my mother and Sophie were already gone. I pushed the letter into Grand Master Kwan's palm, then pulled on my winter coat and followed him and my brother out to his old olive-green Cadillac, which was parked in our unplowed driveway.

In Grand Master Kwan's car, I sat in the back seat. My skin was hot from crying so much. I leaned my head against the cold window and watched the fluctuating height of the snowbanks of last night's plowed blizzard piled on the guard rails. The snow was a muddy beige color and full of rocks.

Looking in his rear-view mirror, in a strong Korean accent Grand Master Kwan said, "You strong."

I pursed my lips together. Crying wasn't going to bring my father back. In my mind I reiterated what my mother said. *God wanted Daddy to come home. The angels came and took him to heaven.* I didn't believe in God. Since my earliest recollections, I'd thought God was a fairytale, which people used to comfort themselves. In Grand Master Kwan's car, I made a conscious effort to maintain my conviction, but to entertain the idea of God, only for the temporary relief of the most anguish I'd ever experienced. For a brief moment, I imagined beautiful lights shining in through my living room window, illuminating my father's body and coaxing his soul into the afterlife. For a moment I relished in such a delicate visualization. I let myself get lost in the fantasy in order to loosen the noose around my heart. A moment later, though, I reminded myself that there was no life after death, and there was no God waiting to greet my father. I forced the notion out of my mind and tried to focus my thoughts on what my mother might be doing without me.

At Grand Master Kwan's house, my brother played with his daughter. Playing with toys didn't appeal to me. For a long time, I sat and waited, longing to be with my mother. I stared out the window and replayed the events of the morning over and over in my mind. *How could this have happened?* I silently questioned. I dropped my head into my hands but made a commitment to myself that I wouldn't cry any more that day.

Eventually my mother called and instructed Grand Master Kwan to drop off my brother at his best friend Peter's house. I was to be dropped off at Emma's house. I didn't want to be separated from my brother. I assumed we would only be at our friend's houses for a couple of hours, and then our mother would come get us.

Emma had been my best friend since kindergarten. By the time we were eleven years old, she and I had been through a lot together. In third grade her parents divorced. Although my mother told me not to ask her about it, Emma and I had discussed every detail of the divorce. She told me about her father's new wife and the abuse her older brother and mother had suffered. I went to private school and Emma went to public school. Despite attending different schools, we still talked about every detail of our lives. Together Emma and I experienced the evolution of cliques, the uncertainty of puberty, and attraction to our first crushes. We witnessed our older siblings drinking alcohol and evaluated our parents' poor decisions. We talked about ghosts and God and dreamed about growing up, having children, and always being there for each other. She was my best friend, and I thought she always would be.

In her basement we played with her dog. She asked me, "Is it okay if I ask you about what happened?"

It was fine, I thought. She could ask anything she wanted. But I didn't have anything to say. It still wasn't real. Then it occurred to me to ask her, "Why didn't you care this morning when I was telling you on the phone?"

"I thought you were saying 'My dog is dead.' I didn't know why you were making such a big deal about it," she paused, thought, and went on. "Remember my dog died last summer? I thought that's what you were saying. I kept thinking about it, though. I didn't know why you were so upset. In second period, over the loudspeaker, I got called down to the office because my mother was there to pick me up, and I immediately realized what you were saying."

2
Promotion Day

On Saturday, two days after my dad died, I looked up from my neatly typed, carefully worded essay. I had written it weeks ago in preparation for this important day. All the students from my martial arts school were sitting cross-legged, intently waiting for my words. This required portion of the promotion test was usually a mundane generalized mantra, where students pondered the discipline that had earned them their black belts. But this was different. I perceived a tremendous feeling of admiration, respect, and condolence from the crowd. Parents peered in from the waiting room. Some cried, some took pictures. My mother was standing in the corner behind a video camera. Grand Master Kwan sat behind a folding table, which was set up at the front of the room, as it always was during promotion tests. The folding table was covered in a green tablecloth, with a pyramid of colorful belts and a notepad, in which Grand Master Kwan recorded the events of the day.

That morning Grand Master Kwan had knelt in front of me at eye-level and told me no one was requiring me to do the promotion test so soon after my dad's death. I insisted, though, that I was prepared and would persevere regardless, in honor of my dad. My mother also tried to deter me. Nothing anyone said was going to stop me.

My eyes followed the lines on the paper. I read one sentence, then looked up, into the compassionate eyes of students I had trained alongside for years. Frustrated, I folded the paper in half and placed it on Grand Master Kwan's table. Instead of reading, I began to preach from my soul. I told the members of my martial arts school about the incredible man my dad was, and how he fought till the very end. I told them how much martial arts meant to him, and that earning his black belt was the most important thing in the world to him, and that because it was so important to him, it was important to me. I told them my training in martial arts gave me the strength to make it through this tragedy and be strong for my family. I recounted a specific night of training with my dad: Class was particularly strenuous; halfway through, I followed my dad outside, into the cool evening air. The skin on his face turned purple and he grunted, snorted, heaved, and wheezed. Sweat streamed down his temples. On his chest, his skin was bright red beneath the opening of his uniform top. He clung to the side of the building, stumbling to regain his composure. I stood before him, afraid that he was on the brink of a medical emergency. But after a couple of minutes, his breathing slowed and quieted. He pulled his shoulder blades together, leveled his chin, and straightened his spine. He told me it was time to go back into class. He told me we never give up, no matter how insurmountable a challenge seems. My dad didn't just say the words. He practiced perseverance, endurance, and indomitable spirit. Leading by example, he showed me what it meant to earn a black belt. I concluded by explaining to my martial arts school that my black belt no longer mattered to me. The only thing that mattered to me was earning my dad's black belt, and becoming the best I could be, so I could make him proud.

My test was flawless. Not only was I the most athletic student in my martial arts school, but I pristinely accomplished innovative techniques, which I creatively crafted for that special event. There was a special kind of focus with me on that day. I was proud each time I heard the snap of boards breaking. I delivered my poomsae without any mistakes, kicked higher than I ever kicked, and kihapped louder than I ever kihapped.

I bowed my head as Grand Master Kwan removed my red belt and tied my black belt around my waist. He spun me around to face the students of my school. He repeated that my dad passed away only two days earlier. He was impressed that I had decided to test, regardless. He told them on the morning of my dad's death, I had given him the most heartfelt, determined letter, and that it was his honor to present me with my dad's black belt. I grinned. That was the only thing I wanted; to make my dad proud would now be the focal point of my life.

I turned back to him and bowed. He handed me my dad's black belt, with gold Korean writing stitched into the ends. The writing spelled out my dad's name and Grand Master Kwan's name.

After the test was over, a barrage of pictures took place. Parents and students shook my hand and bowed to me. There was a cake in the waiting room with red icing. The cake read, "Kristen, Daddy is smiling down on you today."

3
The Service

After my promotion test, I returned to Emma's house. My mother said she still had a lot to do, and I couldn't come home yet. That made me feel dejected, but I also knew I had no choice other than to comply.

When I woke up on Sunday, it was the day of my dad's service. Emma's mom brought me to my house, and I sat alone on the dark green carpet in my bedroom. Slowly, I panned my head around at the music, wrestling, and Disney posters that hung on my walls. I felt relieved to be in my house, but also felt extracted from the feeling that my house was my home. The air felt still. It didn't feel like there was life in the walls. Everything looked the same, but everything felt wrong. I ran my fingers through the fibers of the carpet. The carpet felt like a carpet. I couldn't pinpoint what was missing.

I heard or read somewhere that funerals are supposed to be a celebration of life, and you are not supposed to wear black and mourn. I wanted to celebrate my dad's life. I wanted everyone in the world to know he had been a saint walking this earth, and that I was proud of his life and accomplishments.

I decided to wear bright orange jogging pants and a bright orange tank top, despite the fact that it was February and there was snow on the ground. My dad's sister, Cathy, came in my room. I knew in her mind she was thinking I should change into a black dress, but she didn't try to argue with me. She told me that my sister's friends went to the airport to pick up my sister, and she would meet us at the church. I was relieved that I was going to see my sister. She had been away at college in Florida, and the last time I saw her was during Christmas. I always admired my sister. She was clever, and to me, she seemed incredibly cool. I assumed that she would stay home for a long time, and that having her home would restore the warm feeling my house was suddenly lacking.

We arrived at the church, and I stood outside, under the vast, gray, dreary winter sky while cars pulled into their spots. Familiar faces solemnly walked across the parking lot and into the building. My eyes settled on my sister. She was disheveled, wearing blue sweatpants and a gigantic flannel button-down, buttoned on the wrong buttons and falling off one shoulder. Her hair was unkempt, pulled back with an elastic in a messy bun. The laces of her untied sneakers dragged through frosty puddles on the concrete. Friends linked her arms, holding her up. She was dragging her feet and appeared dazed. I'd never seen her looking like that.

During the service I was surrounded by friends from school, and by Emma. To ease the tension, one of my friends playfully tickled my back. I was really grateful to have them there.

I anticipated a coffin, and that I would see my dad resting peacefully. But someone told me my mother decided to have him cremated. Vivid images of his body being incinerated in a metal box ran through my mind. Because I was distracted by my friends, I was able to turn my attention away from the realization that I would not see my dad resting in a coffin. I wanted to know why he wasn't going to be buried. I also wanted to know exactly what the process for cremation was, but I realized every adult around me was in such a state of devastation that it would have been disrespectful to ask questions.

My grandma, my dad's mother, was to the right of me, sobbing excessively. My aunt and another family friend huddled around her, trying to ease her sorrow. Tissue boxes were being passed around on all sides. I didn't cry. I didn't even feel sad. I just felt a tremendous need to be strong for my family. I tried to comfort my grandma, but her sobbing was an impenetrable, conspicuous wall.

At the end of the service, one of the members of our martial arts school made a beautiful speech. Everyone stood in the lobby of the church, joined hands, and said a prayer. I bowed my head and listened, but also thought about how much I was sure God didn't exist. My other main thought was that I wanted to say something. I wanted to be heard. I wanted everyone to know how much I was hurting, and how scared I was of life moving forward without my dad. But there was never an opportunity for me to speak. No one wanted to hear what an eleven-year-old had to say on the subject of her dad passing away.

People were hugging and wiping away

tears. They were getting in their cars and driving away. I was standing outside of the church looking at the icicles hanging from the gutter. A regal man wearing an expensive coat with large buttons and shiny brown leather shoes approached me.

"Hi, Kristen," he said. "Do you know who I am?"

I shook my head no.

"I'm your godfather," he insisted. "I'm your godfather, Nicholas."

"Where have you been my entire life?" I asked indignantly.

I had always known I had godparents named Nicholas and Gladys. Allegedly they came to my baptism and gave me a gold locket with my initials and the wrong birth date inscribed on it. After that I had never seen them again. I had always felt a little bit jealous that my sister and brother's godparents made the effort to consistently be part of their lives and actually cared about them.

"Well," he started. "I wanted to talk to you about that. I'm sorry I wasn't around before. But I promise from this point on, I am going to be there for you."

"To do what?" I asked.

"To help you as you grow up," he assured. "I'll do whatever you want me to do. I'm going to help pay for your college education, come to your martial arts promotion tests, and see you as often as I can. Is there anything you want right now?"

I thought for a moment. Then I pointed up. "I want one of those." I was pointing to the icicles, which were hanging from the gutter of the church.

Nicholas looked over, then stepped into the deep snow. He extended his arm and snapped off an icicle. He returned and delivered it to me. I smiled, flipped it around, and put it in my mouth. *That'll be nice*, I thought, *to have him around*. I was looking forward to getting to know him. Having a godfather seemed like a really special gift, especially when I was so devastated and felt like I had no one to talk to.

After the service, I never saw Nicholas again.

4
Super Bowl Sunday

In the afternoon, after the service, people came over to our house. I was standing in the arch between the kitchen and the living room. To my left, in the warm light of the kitchen, women were consoling my mother. They were busily unwrapping trays of crackers and cheese, and bowls of fruit salad, and boxes of sandwiches. My grandma's hollow shell was sitting at the kitchen table, staring at nothing and slowly rocking back and forth. My Aunt Cathy, her daughter, caressed her back while politely thanking the other ladies chattering around the table. My Aunt Beth, who was my mother's sister, was at the stove cooking her famous red sauce. To my right, in the dim living room, the only light that came in was through the undrawn shades of the window. Uncles, my sister's male friends, and my dad's friends were standing around silently and somberly. They were holding beers, and staring at the giant projection television, which was black. I looked back to the ladies in the kitchen, and there was a rise in chatter. But the men in the living room remained in somber silence and sadness.

My mother walked into the living room holding a tray of sandwiches. All the men looked up in unison.

"It's okay," my mother said. "You can turn the TV on."

Suddenly the men perked up. One of my sister's friends bent down to push the power button. He hesitated for a moment, looked back at the other men, then pressed the button. The TV powered on and someone picked up the remote control. They clicked the channel twice, and all at once, the men let out a roaring cheer. They settled onto the couches, and someone went downstairs to get extra chairs.

The Super Bowl was on.

I stood there and looked at them. Several of them were sitting on the couch, right where my dad died. They were nestled right on top of that sacred final resting place and they didn't care. They were just cheering for their team.

I retreated again into my parents' bedroom. I wanted to be alone. I closed the door and sat on the bed. I thought for a moment about the phone call I had made to Emma, and how I sat there crying, and how she couldn't understand me.

I went in my parent's closet and saw my dad's vacation hat on the top shelf. I piled up some boxes and climbed up to snatch it down. It was a straw Panama Jack hat with a band of fabric featuring colorful tropical flowers. I set the hat on their bed. I went in their dresser and found a giant pair of my dad's favorite sweatpants. I laid them on the bed too. I went back into the closet. I ran my fingers through the fabric of the different hanging garments, and eventually settled on the slick material of my father's winter coat. I held it to my face and breathed in his scent. I realized that this would eventually disappear completely, and I needed to find a way to preserve as much of him as I could.

I put on his jacket, pulled the sweatpants up around my waist, and set his hat on top of my head. I looked back toward the closet and saw his sneakers. I slipped those on too. Surrounded by my father's clothes, my arms full of excess fabric, I shuffled into the hallway. I stood there for a moment. My tiny frame was enveloped. I watched people reach for snacks on the table. I listened to the men in the living room cheer for a touchdown. I really didn't feel like having a party. I wasn't hungry and wasn't in the mood to watch television. I didn't understand how anyone could want those things.

My Aunt Cathy was bringing a tray from the kitchen into the living room when she walked past and saw me standing there in the hallway. She stopped and her mouth dropped open as her gaze settled on me. She spun around and muttered something to someone sitting at the kitchen table. I darted to my left and went into the bathroom. I shut the door and pressed the lock. I sat down on the toilet, drew my knees into my chest, and pulled the jacket up around my face. For the first time since the phone call with Emma, I sobbed. I breathed my father in and breathed out my soul. I cried out to the universe to take the pain away, and bring my father home where he belonged.

I heard some rattling, then the ping of the lock getting picked. I peeked up out of the jacket. Through blurry, teary eyes I could see my mother standing in the door frame. Both my aunts and family friends were crowded behind her, peering over her shoulders. I felt on display. The grief was overwhelming and I only wanted to breathe my father in deeper. I was angry that they picked the lock. My mother looked empty. I think she was so consumed by her own grief that she couldn't even begin to process the pain of her children. She stood in the door frame for several moments, then hung her head and turned away. Aunt Cathy watched her walk back to the kitchen, and then looked back to me. She came into the bathroom and knelt down, so that she was below the brim of the hat. She looked deep into the pain in the eyes. She pulled me in close to hug me for a moment, then stood up, turned to the women standing in the doorway and said, "It's just so sad," as she followed them back into the kitchen, leaving me alone on the toilet.

5

You Don't Understand

My brother and I were sitting in a stark, meagerly decorated room with white walls and folding tables configured in a 'U' shape. There were stacks of colorful construction paper and plastic bins of half-used crayons on the tables, all muted by the obnoxious flicker of fluorescent lights. The curtains were pulled down, blocking out the mid-February afternoon sun. Paper plates crafted into mutilated faces and cheap finger paint handprints configured like flowers were taped to the walls. Instead of making the room more cheerful, they made the room look like a sterile daycare center for the mentally disturbed.

Even though my dad died only a couple days ago, I felt like I hadn't seen my mother in months. The entire time I was at Emma's house I wanted to go home. But my mother said she had things to do. *What was more important than being with your children immediately after a tragedy?* I imagined there must have been mountains of required paperwork after someone dies, and that when she completed that, she would have wise, loving, endearing, compassionate words to say to me that would take my pain away.

I always knew that my mother's mother died when she was nine years old. It was a tragedy I felt disconnected from. It was like hearing about the war at Gettysburg. I knew it was important, but in the selfish way children think, it didn't directly affect me. My mother never talked about it very much. I knew it happened, but I didn't know anything about the woman who was my grandmother. I'd never seen a picture of her, visited the house my mother grew up in, or saw anything that belonged to my grandmother. I didn't know how she died and didn't know what happened to my mother after her mother was gone. But still, I knew it happened, and never thought it might happen to me. I thought my mother might sit me down one day soon and recount her experience and tell me how long it might take for the pain to go away.

Two women spoke kindly, instructing children who filtered into the room to take their seats. One of the women stood at the front of the room. Motioning toward my brother and I, she said we were new additions to the program, and everyone should try to make us feel welcome. I looked around and realized that the group of children's median age was at least four years younger than mine. The women asked the children to introduce themselves and, if they felt comfortable, explain why they were there. One by one, each child candidly volunteered their name, and explained that their aunt or grandfather, or their mother's friend who they were really close to died. My immediate reaction was irritation. *Who the hell were these kids? Did they really have the audacity to try to compare the loss of my father to the loss of their aunt?* I felt betrayed, angry, and disrespected. No matter how much these kids loved their grandfathers, it completely paled in comparison to how much I loved my dad.

For several weeks we continued to go to these group art-therapy sessions. I was a very artistic and creative child. At a very young age I understood the concept of emotion through art. I had a genuine appreciation, by the time I was in third grade, for different mediums. I loved thick acrylic paint. I would spend hours meticulously detailing sketches born in the depths of my imagination. I would sit cross-legged on the playground and sketch while my classmates stood over my shoulders commenting on the strange content of my drawings. A common school project we were required to complete was shadow boxes. We had to read a book, then recreate a scene from the book in a shoebox. My shadow boxes were always the most detailed and put on display in the lobby of our school for a month. I truly loved and excelled in art.

At the art therapy group, we were stapling fringe to baseball caps. This was fucking stupid. This was a waste of my fucking time.

The kids in the program were so happy to be doing arts and crafts. They were happy to chat about Pokémon and their favorite TV shows. They were excited that someone was complimenting their stapling and glitter-glue abilities.

This wasn't art. These kids weren't grieving. They were playing. My life was fucking destroyed. My dad, the most important person in the world, was gone, and we were gluing string to neon poster board.

I felt so unheard.

My mother barely spoke to us. I wanted answers. I wanted to know the plan for moving forward. I wanted my dad to just come home. I wanted to know how to preserve him. I wanted to know how to remember every freckle on his skin and every story he ever told me.

I needed real therapy. I needed help processing what had happened. I needed stability, patience, and kindness. Mostly, I needed guidance. I hated going to the art therapy sessions. I hated hearing what the other children had to say about their aunt or their grandfather, mainly because I knew that both their mom and dad were going to tuck them into bed at night. I felt like the sessions were a complete waste of time.

On what would be my brother's and my last day going to the art-therapy sessions, a teenage girl with mousy, medium-length hair was standing in the hallway. I noticed her, but she was a little bit older than me, and I didn't think her presence had any relevance to me, so I didn't think too much about her. I went into the room and sat at the table. My brother sat to the left of me. I was relieved that it was our last day.

The counselors asked for everyone to settle

down, and then the girl came into the room. They introduced her and told us she used to attend this program, and they were glad that she came to visit.

"Who died?" I bluntly asked her.

I expected her to say it was her aunt or her grandfather. I felt like so much of my time had been wasted, I didn't see the point in wasting anymore of it. Within seconds I devised a myriad of snarky, immature, rude things to say to this girl.

She responded, "My brother."

In shock, I drew my head back and held in my breath. I shifted uncomfortably in the seat. I looked to my left. My brother was my best friend. *Brothers don't die. Old people die. My dad wasn't old, but he wasn't a kid. Kids don't die.*

She continued, "He drowned last summer. We were camping, and everyone had gone to sleep. No one knows how it happened, but in the middle of the night, my brother got out of the tent. No one woke up. No one remembers hearing anything."

"How old was he?" I squeaked out.

She answered, "Eight."

I swallowed hard. My brother was ten years old, and I could not imagine losing him. Even though my dad just died, I couldn't fathom losing my brother. Meeting that girl made me feel like I wasn't completely alone in my agony. I wished that she had been part of the sessions, instead of the younger children, who were obviously not deeply impacted by their losses. I was so rattled by her story that I couldn't think of anything else to ask her. I wish I had had more time with her.

~before~

6

Soulmates

One evening, when I was three years old, I sat at the kitchen table swinging my little legs, which weren't quite long enough to touch the floor. My mother was at the stove rolling meatballs. I could smell the oil and garlic heating in the pan. My father came in and put his arms around my mother's waist, kissing her neck and drawing a long deep breath in. My mother turned, holding her hands out to the sides, because there was ground beef and egg on them. My father pulled her in closer. He very passionately gave her a long, deep kiss.

He turned to me and said, "I know your mother is my soulmate because every time I kiss her, my head spins."

I smiled.

7

Margret

The TV flickered, creating a dim blue glow. I was a sleepy-eyed toddler lying face down on my babysitter Margret's dusty old tweed couch. My body felt heavy and stiff.

Abruptly, her hand gripped the back of my neck. Her fingers stabbed my fragile skin. She shoved my head into the cushion and leaned all of her weight onto my neck. My tiny body struggled under the pressure. I thought she was going to squeeze my head off!

"What the fuck did you do?" she sputtered in my ear.

She smelled stale. The smell choked me. I had no idea what I had done.

She yanked my hair and pulled me off the couch. I struggled to keep up as she dragged me across the house. In the bathroom I was directed to sit on the toilet. Cold urine soaked my feety pajamas, sticking the fabric to my legs. My muscles pulsed. My tears burned the cuts her fingernails left on my neck.

I cried on the toilet for a long time but

didn't move.

She came in, beer bottle in one hand, spray bottle in the other.

"Clean it up," she sneered at me.

I looked up at her, petrified and confused. She looked down at me, glaring with hatred. I didn't know how to use a spray bottle. I only recognized it as something my mother always cautioned me to stay away from. I felt stupid and trapped.

She motioned harshly and I made my way back to the couch. Standing in front of the wet spot, I peered down the nozzle and squeezed the trigger. Pain shot through my eyeballs. Tears flooded out. I choked, I couldn't breathe. My nose ran. I flailed my arms, smacked at my face, panicking.

"You retard!" she shouted. She grabbed me by my arm and yanked me across the house. I could hear the sound of water running in the bathroom. Still wearing my urine-soaked feety pajamas, she hoisted me into the bathtub, which was half-full of ice-cold water. She left for a moment. I scooped up water and splashed it in my eyes, not knowing the introduction of urine would hurt. My eyes immediately burned, another shocking jolt of pain went through me. The taste of chemicals permeated my throat and burned my esophagus.

When she came back, she stood me up and peeled off my soaked pajamas. She held my head under the faucet. I struggled to break from her grip. I couldn't breathe. I was drowning. I was inhaling water. I was choking on chemicals and urine.

She finally let me go. She stood up, took a sip of her beer, and looked down at me with disgust. I looked up at her shivering from fear, adrenaline, and the icy water I was still standing in. She finished the bottle, tossed it in the sink, and dragged me out of the tub. Still crying and choking and trembling, she wiped the water off my skin, the towel like sandpaper, and put an oversized shirt on me. My arms ached as I lifted them into the sleeves. She dragged me up the stairs and dropped me into a mobile pack-and-play.

Through the mesh walls and my tears, I watched as she left the room.

I whimpered and lay there and choked. I vomited on one side of the pack-and-play. The smell was awful, and my nostrils and throat were raw. I continued to cough up the acidic chemical particles still lodged inside me. I moved to the other side of the pack-and-play. I continued to cry until I fell asleep.

When I woke up, I had been moved to Margret's king-sized bed. I was dressed in my feety pajamas, which smelled of fabric softener. My beloved baby blanky was in my arms. My stomach felt empty and my eyelids sore.

"Rise and shine, sweetheart," Margret cooed. "Are you ready for a snack?"

I gripped my blanky in fear. She picked me up and I recoiled. She turned and sat on the bed, holding me in her lap. "There, there," she said. I didn't trust her.

She carried me into the living room. *The Rugrats* were on television. I trembled as I let cold apple sauce and milk soothe my throat and fall, like a brick, into my traumatized stomach.

When my daddy arrived, I bolted to the door. I locked onto his leg. In my short life I had never been more relieved to see him. I wanted to tell him what had happened, but I was so ecstatic about his presence that I couldn't do anything but grip his leg with all four of my limbs.

Margret recited a detailed story for my daddy, which she must have prepared while I was asleep. She told him I was sick, probably with an eye infection. She said she didn't think it was serious enough to go to the hospital and that it would probably clear up in a couple days. She reminded him about her years as a nurturing childcare provider, and that she'd seen plenty of children with this type of eye infection in the past. Toward the end of her appeal, she reiterated that a doctor wouldn't be able to do anything, and rest would be the only remedy.

My dad picked me up and looked into my eyes. He frowned, because my eyes were bloodshot and puffy. He asked me if I was okay. I nodded. He carried me out the door and we went home.

A week went by. My eyes cleared up. I didn't seem sick.

My dad put my helmet on and put me on the back of his motorcycle. Wind sucked up through the bottom of the helmet and felt good on my face. As instructed many times before, I held onto my dad's waist tightly. I didn't know where we were going. I was just happy to be close to him.

As soon as we got to Margret's house, I was panic-stricken. I gripped onto the bar on the back of my dad's motorcycle and wouldn't let go. I cried and I kicked and I screamed. My dad pried me from the bar. I clung to him, crying and screaming as loud as I could.

"Sometimes they're like that," Margret said to my dad.

That was the last time I ever saw Margret.

8

Lies Before Kindergarten

I was holding my mother's hand as the winter sun was setting. It was brisk. Cool air penetrated my jacket. She was walking me across a parking lot.

"You're going to be a big girl, right?" She looked down at me.

I nodded, not sure where we were or why we were there.

We walked through automatic double doors, and I realized we were in a hospital, but I didn't understand why.

I was sitting in a chair, getting my temperature and blood pressure taken.

I was in a hospital bed, screaming, "Blanky, blanky, where is my blanky?"

"Kristy," my mother said to me. "Grandma and Daddy are looking for your blanky, and they'll bring it soon, I promise. I need you to be a big girl. You have to get some shots."

"Why?" I hollered. *Why was this happening*

to me? What did I do to deserve this nightmare?

"All the kids who are going into kindergarten have to get shots. If you don't get them, you won't be able to start school," my mother reasoned with me.

While the idea of starting kindergarten in six months was the most exciting thing that had ever happened to me, the notion that shots were required was a deal breaker.

A doctor came in, and a nurse held me down and they put an IV in my arm. I cried and called out for my blanky.

I was lying in the hospital bed when my grandma came in. From a white plastic bag, she pulled out a pink, plush bunny rabbit that was as big as my body, and a blanky made of felt. *What the hell is this?* I thought to myself. I began to cry. "Blanky, blanky, where is blanky?" I did not want this impostor blanky.

"We couldn't find blanky. Grandma got you a new blanky." My mother thanked my grandmother, but I was furious. Not only was I in horrible pain, but they lost my beloved blanky. After a few moments, though, I calmed down and felt this sense of obligation to be thankful for my grandmother's efforts, so I held the bunny close, but could not betray my one and only blanky by accepting this ugly, heavy, itchy impostor blanky, so I pushed it to the far end of the bed.

"Where's Charles?" my mother asked my grandmother. "He should be here by now."

Yeah, I thought, *where's my dad? He won't disappoint me. He'll come with blanky.*

"He left the house with Stefanie right after I left," my grandma said.

My mother picked up the phone next to me and dialed our house number. There was no answer. My grandma picked up the phone and dialed a different number. Still no answer. My mother took the phone from her, and punched in more numbers.

My grandma opened a container of red Jell-O for me. I watched my mother dial the phone again, then dial our neighbor's number.

"Stay here with Kristy," my mother instructed my grandmother.

My mother got up, kissed me, and left.

After a long time of watching cartoons and eating Jell-O, a nurse came in to talk to my grandma. My grandma sprung up and left the room. Everyone was gone.

Why would they abandon me? I asked myself. I felt isolated, unwanted, and numb to everything except the pain of the IV in my arm. I recoiled, feeling really sorry for myself. I cried into the pink bunny my grandma had given me until I felt a hand on my shoulder. I looked up into the kind eyes of a nurse.

"Your mother and grandmother will be right back, I promise. I will wait with you until they come," the kind nurse reassured me.

I dried my tears and was grateful the nurse was there.

A long time after, my mother came in and told me my dad had gotten in a car accident with my sister. They were on their way to see me, when the car skidded and flipped on black ice. She said my sister was okay, but my dad was hurt, and had to stay in the hospital in a different room. I wanted my dad to stay in the same room as me. My mother said the hospital had a policy against children and adults staying in the same room. That seemed really stupid to me.

9

Sugar

We'd been driving for hours, and finally arrived at a house in the woods. My dad turned the car off, and my mother opened the sliding door of the minivan. I stood beside a deep snowbank. The chimney of the house puffed out black smoke. My dad led the way, over a shoveled gravel path with four feet of snow piled up on each side. Two brown and tan German Shepherds were chained to a dog house, frantically barking at us.

"Aren't they cold?" I asked my sister, Stefanie.

Stefanie said, "No, they're bred to be outside like that. These people raise a lot of dogs. They know exactly what they're doing."

We stood in the mud room while my father went into the living room. After a moment of talking, the rest of us were invited inside.

A lady in the house whistled, and this fat, white unbelievably adorable furry blob came waddling toward us. My dad scooped it up, and we followed him outside. I was in shock. I couldn't believe it! We got a puppy! She was the cutest thing I had ever seen. He held her over his shoulder like a baby and sang "A-doomp-a-doomp-a-puppy-a-doomp-a-doomp-a-baby-dog."

In the car everyone was gleeful, chattering about what to name her. Eventually we settled on Sugar, because she had white fur.

My parents told us the German Shepherds that were outside were her parents, and that she was the only puppy in the litter, and it was a coincidence that she had been born white. I felt sad for them. I wondered if they were going to miss their baby.

Back at home my dad specifically told us not to let Sugar outside, because it had just snowed, and he didn't want her to get lost.

One morning my brother opened the front door and the puppy went barreling out.

"No!" My father shouted. He catapulted off the couch. Without even putting shoes on he ran out the front door and into the snow.

A minute later he came back in with the puppy tucked under one arm.

"She could suffocate out there. She's too small to get her head above the snow," he said to us.

As the puppy grew, she became inseparable from my dad. My dad was really stern with her and trained her with an iron fist. She became an excellent family dog but was always immeasurably loyal to my dad.

10

Wake Up

My parents worked in New York City and were afraid that if my sister, brother, or I got sick during the day, they'd be too far away to come pick us up. Every day, for the year my brother was in kindergarten, I was in first grade, and my sister was in eighth grade, my parents would wake up at 4:30 a.m., load their sleeping children in the car, and battle New York City rush hour traffic to bring us to a private Catholic school in Greenwich Village.

It was dark out, chilly, and there was dew in the air.

"A-doomp-a-doomp-a-Kristy-a-doomp-a-doomp-a-baby-girl…" my father was singing while he cradled me in a blanket, holding me close to his chest, and carried me down the hill. He placed me in a bed he had made in the back of our purple minivan, where my brother and sister were already sleeping. I lay down, heard the passenger's door shut, and heard my mother say something to my dad as I faded away.

I woke up and saw a building in the woods, which I assumed was the beginning of the city. I imagined the city and the mountains of New Jersey to be a gradient that blended together in a porous way. On the radio I could hear Howard Stern's monotone voice talking about nothing I cared about, so I drifted back to sleep.

I woke up again, this time parallel parked on a side street in Manhattan. In the back of the van my mother helped me into my green plaid uniform. My sister sat in the front seat eating a bagel. My brother hung his feet out the driver's side while my dad finished buttoning his son's white shirt and attached his green clip-on tie.

I held my sister's hand and my brother held her other one. She led us down the block and I watched over my shoulder. My parents pulled out of their parking spot and the purple minivan disappeared into New York City's morning traffic.

Groggy, I climbed the stairs up to my first grade classroom and took my seat at my desk. My teacher was a stern, malicious woman with a chiseled face, and I was scared of her. But there was something inside me that always wanted to impress her. Month after month I tried to color within the lines, read clearly, and add faster. Nothing I did was ever good enough. I couldn't win her approval. I would stare over her shoulder at the crucifix and lament in my mind how frustrated I was.

She had a method of dividing the classroom into three sections, then giving busy work to two of the sections while she taught the third section. She would have the students rotate through the sections, so at certain times we would switch desks.

A boy named Zachary sat in my desk while I was on the other side of the room. At one point during the lesson, our teacher began screaming at him because he had committed an unforgivable atrocity; he'd stammered while reading. He sank low in the chair, wanting to disappear. I felt bad for him, knowing he must have been very embarrassed. All our eyes rested upon him pityingly.

Our teacher was finished with his section and told us to rotate.

I stood up and walked over to my desk, which Zachary had previously occupied. I looked down and there was a puddle dripping off both the front and back of the seat. I began to feel anxious because I knew everyone had taken their seats, and I would be in trouble if I didn't sit down.

I looked up and started, "Um, Mrs.—"

But the teacher sneered at me, "Unless you're dying, you better sit down right now."

I looked back at the wet seat. I swallowed a lump in my throat and tried to sit only on the edge of the seat.

"*Sit!*" she roared.

I started to cry.

Full of fury she stormed over to me, ready to scream at me. Right as she opened her mouth, drew in a deep breath, and extended her arm to shove me into the seat, she looked down. She stopped. "Oh..." she sneered. She turned her burning eyes to Zachary. He was on the other side of the room, shriveled into another desk. I breathed a sigh of relief for myself, but then immediately felt dread for the wrath Zachary was about to endure.

The next day our teacher called the class to attention. "I have an announcement to make," she started, "Zachary has left our school. Does anyone want his dinosaur coloring book?"

I raised my hand, and she passed it to me.

That day I opened the coloring book, thumbed through the pages, and breathed in the remains of the memory of that child. I was happy for him, that he had escaped the hell I was still living in.

Like most children, my favorite part of the day, of course, was recess. It was my only opportunity to escape the daily torment of our callous teacher. Our school would use police barricades to block off a section of the street, which is where we would play.

One day we came down the stairs, excited to dart outside. The principal stood in the doorway and said we couldn't go out, and had to have recess in our classroom for the next couple days.

Disappointed, we turned around and headed back to our classroom. Upstairs I pressed my face against the glass, longing to be outside, wishing for some space away from my mean teacher. I was confused, because the street was blocked off, but there were white vans and people outside. *Why can't they just move?* I thought to myself.

Years later I found out that they were filming a scene from *Men in Black* where an alien kills two old men in a restaurant. Filming took a week, and we weren't allowed to go outside to play the entire time.

My dad came to get us from school. My mother had to stay at work a little longer than expected. I was really excited to see him, and to show him off to my friends. I pulled him by his hand around our classroom. He wore dusty tan work boots, jeans, and a stained white T-shirt that said the name of the company he worked for on the pocket.

When we left school, my dad carried me on his shoulders. I wore his hard hat and stabilized myself on his forehead. He held my brother's hand and carried my sister's backpack in the other.

My sister talked to him about a complicated science project. I smiled, because my dad was so brilliant, and I knew he'd be able to help her. We stood at an intersection waiting to cross the street, and a man came up behind my dad.

"Spare change?" the homeless man requested.

My dad ignored him and continued talking to my sister.

"Yo, man," the homeless man said in an agitated voice. "Don't fuckin' ignore me!"

My dad turned back to the man, and while lifting me off his shoulders and placing me on the sidewalk next to my brother and sister, my dad said, "Look at you. Your sneakers are more expensive than mine."

My dad took our hands and led us across the street. I looked back at the man, whose head hung low, staring at his brand new white Jordans. I looked down at my dad's dusty, old, worn-out work boots, which were disconnecting from the soles, and had paint and grime splattered on them. Then I looked at my own shoes, which were clean, shiny, black dress shoes, over my white knee-high socks. My sister and brother also wore clean, shiny, black dress shoes. In that moment I realized how much my dad sacrificed to send us to private Catholic school.

Kneeling down to be eye-level with us, my dad said, "Don't ever give money to anyone wearing shoes more expensive than yours."

He stood up and continued walking us down the street. We reached a brick building with beautiful stone steps. We followed my dad into the building, up an elevator, and into a doctor's office. We waited in the waiting room for a long time. Eventually my mother came. She said hello, and then went to the receptionist, who led her back to meet my dad.

Some time later my dad had to have surgery. My mother led us into the hospital. She warned us that my dad wouldn't be able to speak to us.

When we turned the corner and entered the room, my dad sat upright and grinned. We each ran up to him and hugged him tightly. My mother explained that my dad had been diagnosed with Sleep Apnea and had a surgery to cut all the excess skin out of the back of his throat to help him breathe better when he slept. She said he couldn't speak now, but would get better and come home in two days.

When my dad came home he had a breathing machine that he had to wear at night. It was big, and sounded really scary. I was relieved when he started talking again, and I hoped his Sleep Apnea had been cured.

11

Bath Time

"Grandma!" I catapulted toward the door. I was thrilled! I hadn't seen her in such a long time.

"Hi, Little Cookie!" She stretched out her arms and lifted me up. I was so happy to be held by her.

My grandma came into the house and Sugar, our German Shepherd, began making this low, grumbly, growling kind of noise toward my grandma. We'd never heard that noise before.

"Sug!" my dad snapped.

She didn't stop. My dad got off the couch and dragged the dog into the master bedroom. When he came back out, he said, "Maybe there's a thunderstorm coming. I don't know why she's acting aggressive."

"I have something special for you," my grandma cooed to me. "It's out in the car still."

I squealed with delight, then I followed her out the front door, down the steps, and onto the driveway. I looked up at the sky and noticed there wasn't a single cloud. From her car she gave me a bouquet of silk flowers. "They'll never die," she said. I absolutely loved them. I took them in the house and set them on my dresser, so that I would be able to see them from my bed.

I was standing up in the bathtub. Warm water pooled around my ankles. My grandma was kneeling next to the tub, looking at me eye-level, holding the detachable shower head with one hand and washing my body with the other.

She began washing my vagina.

"It burns, Grandma!" I cried to her, trying to pull away.

She didn't stop. She said, "That's just the soap disinfecting you."

12

The BQE

My dad was driving my mother, my brother, my sister, and me in our purple minivan. My brother and I were safely strapped into our booster seats playing with our Happy Meal toys, and my sister was lying across the third row of seats with headphones on, listening to music on her Walkman. Her seat belt was buckled, but because of how she was lying, it wasn't really protecting her. We were on the BQE in the beginning of aggressive New York City rush hour traffic.

A small white car swerved and cut my dad off. He slammed on the brakes, missing a collision by inches, then ferociously accelerated, nearly pushing the white car into the concrete wall.

"Charles!" my mother screeched.

The other driver stuck his head and middle finger out of the window, screaming back at my father. In a rage, my dad stuck his head out, furiously screaming back.

The white car pulled over to the shoulder

and my dad pulled up behind it, about twenty feet away. My dad's massive frame bolted out of the minivan, and with the precision and tenacity of a bull, sprinted toward the white car. The white car's door swung open. My father leaped into the air, twisted to the side and flying side-kicked the man's car door. It made a loud cracking sound and the door bent all the way backward, flush against the fender. My dad reached into the car, and all I could see was the man's legs. My father was trying to drag him out of the car, but he was gripping his steering wheel for dear life.

Panicking, my mother shouted, "Stay here!" as she shuffled out of our car and ran up behind my dad.

We watched as my mother tried to pull my dad off the man. Cars began slowing down to rubberneck and see the fight. Because of my mother's pleading, my dad finally dropped the man's legs and turned to walk toward the minivan. I saw the man scurry into the car and the tires chirped as he peeled down the shoulder. His car door was still bent against his fender and was making a banging sound.

My dad got back in the driver's seat and pulled back into the mounting traffic. Not too far up the road, we saw the man standing outside of his car, staring at the damage my dad's flying side-kick had done to his car. He looked completely bewildered and full of anxiety.

My parents were talking and my dad said, "With my family in the car? I wouldn't have reacted like that if it were just me. But with my kids and my wife? No. He got what he had coming to him."

13
The Most Perfect Evening

It was my sixth birthday, and we had driven down to Florida for vacation. We were on the beach in Key Largo and the sun was setting, turning the sky a palette of bright oranges and pinks. There were small gentle waves rhythmically crashing onto the sand. I sat beneath a cabana made of dried palm fronds, which crinkled as the warm breeze blew through them. The beach was deserted in both directions.

At any beach we went to, my dad would help us build sharks in the sand. Because my brother and I were little, we'd do the heavy lifting, and pile sand into a long mound. We'd help our dad smooth out the sides, and fetch saltwater in our plastic buckets. We'd watch our dad sculpt the shark, then carefully drizzle fine sand mixed with saltwater to make the fins. Our dad would spray paint the whole thing gray, and then use white shells to fashion the teeth, and shiny black rocks to create the eyes. Our dad would drag either me or my brother from the ocean to the shark to leave track marks, which made it appear like he dragged the shark out of the ocean. Other beachgoers would frequently approach us and ask to take a picture with the shark. We were always happy to take their pictures.

On that evening, though, all the beachgoers had gone home. My dad stood up from the shark and I watched him pull the sleeves of his wet suit over his arms, then hoist his scuba tank onto his back. Wearing his fins, he took big, awkward steps into the ocean.

My sister was seated at a wooden picnic table tuning the radio, and my mother was getting a bag of charcoal from the car. My brother and I dug our feet into the sand when I looked back over to spot my dad. He was waist deep in the ocean. He put his respirator in his mouth, put one hand to his goggles, swung his other arm back, and dove into the next wave. His fins splashed the ocean water up until he disappeared completely.

There was a fire. My mother, dad, and sister were cleverly stacking dried coral, and cleverly balancing a metal grate on top. My dad pulled raw lobster tails out of his pockets, and my mother and my sister started laughing.

My dad had gone into the ocean and chased lobsters, yanked off their tails, then came up to the beach, and we sat around a fire and roasted them on sticks. I asked why he didn't bring the whole bodies, and he said we didn't need the bodies, and that lobsters can survive without their tails, and that their tails would grow back. He also explained that Florida lobsters have no natural predators, so they don't have claws.

We ate lobster until we couldn't eat anymore. In my life I had never felt so full or warm as I did in that moment.

That night we piled into our purple minivan. My brother and I quickly fell asleep. When we woke up, we were in Boca Raton at my brother's godparents' house. Our parents carried us inside and I fell back asleep on the cool leather couch in the living room.

In the morning I woke up, delighted to see my cousins. Bright Florida sun was beaming through the windows. I went to the kitchen where my Aunt Maria was making coffee.

"Where's my mom and dad?" I asked her.

She turned to me, leaned over the counter, and said, "Your mom had to go out. She'll be back soon. What would you like for breakfast?"

Aunt Maria busily started making pancakes and bacon, and I went in my cousin's room to play with her Barbies.

I heard the car door shut and excitedly made my way to the front door. I pulled open the heavy wooden door, expecting to see both of my parents. I stood in the frame and watched my mother, whose long hair hung over her shoulders, stare at the ground.

"Hi Kristy, baby." She sounded meek.

"Where's Daddy?" I asked.

She let out a sigh and said, "Daddy had to go back to work. We're going to stay in Florida for a little while."

I felt disappointed. But her explanation made sense, and I was happy to be on vacation. I followed her into the house. My aunt and cousins were setting the table for breakfast. When all of the children were seated with their pancakes cut in bite-sized squares and orange juice poured, my aunt and mother disappeared into the master bedroom and shut the door.

I didn't think anything else of it. When we

were done eating, we left the dishes on the table and resumed our game in my cousin's bedroom.

14

Man Hole

A month later, back home, my sister, brother, and I were seated around our kitchen table eating breakfast. The screen door was open, letting in a lovely May morning breeze. I thought, *New Jersey is so beautiful in the spring time*. My mother had planted petunias and marigolds on our deck, and I thought she did such a nice job.

My dad, who was working overtime on a Saturday, hadn't come home the night before and my mother was very nervous. It was late in the morning on Sunday when I watched her frantically snap into the phone at a woman who worked in the office of my dad's company.

"They don't know where he is. He never came back with the work truck," my mother said to my sister. "We have to go look for him."

We got in the purple minivan. I sensed that something was very wrong, and my mother was fearing the absolute worst. My dad's current job site was in an upscale area of office buildings. Because it was Sunday the neatly landscaped parking lot was mostly empty, except for a stray car here and there.

We drove around each building until finally we spotted the work truck. My mother motored toward it. Her eyes were fixed, and she seemed to be organizing thoughts, which she paired with different situations she imagined could have occurred.

"Stay here," she said over her shoulder as she slipped out of the minivan. She crept cautiously toward the work truck, when suddenly she sped up, toward an exposed manhole. She bent down on her knees, talking into the hole.

My sister, brother, and I got out of the car and ran up to the manhole.

"They forgot about me! Those morons left me down here all night!" my dad said to my mother.

My mother instructed us, "Stay here with Dad. I'm going to find a ladder."

"How did they forget about you?" I asked.

"I don't know," he responded.

"Can I come down?" I asked while dangling my feet down the hole.

He extended his arms and gripped around my ankles, "Let go, I'll catch you."

I did, and he did. It was dark and my dad

was standing in six inches of black water. The air in the manhole was wet and cool, and the walls looked slimy. I didn't want to touch anything.

"What were you doing down here?" I asked him.

"You see those cables?" he pointed to colorful cables with black zip ties around them, "It's my job to run them, but my crew left me here all night. I tried to climb out, but there was no way. I thought I was going to be trapped here until Monday."

After a while my dad lifted me into my sister's arms, and my sister pulled me back above ground. My sister, brother, and I sat on the edge of the manhole talking to our dad, whose eyes were bloodshot and was weary from standing for so long. My dad told us about his job, and about the idiots he worked with. Eventually my mother returned with some plastic milk crates. My dad stacked them up, then my mother and sister hoisted my father out of the manhole. Immediately my father untied and removed his work boots and socks, and left them in the grass.

Collapsing in the front seat, my dad said, "Let's go home. I'll deal with this tomorrow."

15

New School

For a lot of reasons, commuting to the city wasn't working. I kept getting in trouble for falling asleep during the day. My parents decided to look for a new school, but determined it was important for us to still attend private Catholic school.

"Do they want them to be pilgrims?" my grandma, who was sitting at our kitchen table, joked as I walked down the hallway wearing my new navy-blue school uniform. It was too big.

My mother came over and pulled at it. "It needs to be hemmed, but she'll grow into it."

The idea of a new school was very appealing to me. I was glad my cruel first-grade teacher was out of my life. I hoped that attending school in New Jersey meant I would get home early enough to have a couple of hours of sunlight left to play with my next-door neighbors.

Because of my parent's work schedule, my brother and I had to take a bus with high-school students; then when we got to their high school, we had to transfer onto a smaller bus with half a dozen children who were our age. I would always fall asleep, and one of the high-school students would abruptly wake me up each morning. I would stumble from the big bus to the small bus, then fall asleep again.

My second-grade teacher was kind. Her name was Mrs. Wellington. She was older than my mother. She had a soft, round face with high cheek bones and beautiful shoulder-length light-blonde hair. I loved her. She had a maternal glow about her. On more than one occasion I accidentally called her 'Mommy.'

The principal's name was Mrs. O'Haver. She was a white-haired, malicious Irish-Catholic woman with a gaunt face and chiseled jawline who burned maleficence toward almost every child in the school. The only exceptions were children whose parents were employed by the school and a few others whose parents made large financial donations. Our regular teacher taught us most subjects. To break up the days, we had a gym teacher who was very fun, an art teacher who was always creative and cheerful, and Mrs. O'Haver, who taught math to each of the grades, from first to eighth.

Every student dreaded math class. Mrs. O'Haver would scream at us until we cried. Mrs. Wellington always did her best to diffuse Mrs. O'Haver's rage.

I developed incredible anxiety about going to school. Though only in second grade, my anxiety would keep me awake until the early hours of the morning. I would frequently wake up screaming from nightmares. At school I would constantly get sent to the nurse's office because I couldn't stay awake in class. I always felt like that made Mrs. O'Haver hate me even more.

16

Christmas Pageant

Our fourth-grade class was tasked with being mice for the Christmas pageant in the auditorium of a high school nearby. We practiced our song for weeks, and in art class we made mouse ears out of construction paper for our big night. Our song was the opening song of the play, and we were sternly reminded not to mess it up.

I was excited, sitting with my class, as parents were filtering in and finding seats in the auditorium.

My sister and her boyfriend walked in right before the show was about to start, and I could tell they weren't able to find my mother and my dad. I stood up and lifted my right arm.

"Mommy and Daddy are over there," I said in a loud whisper as I pointed to a far corner of the auditorium.

Mrs. O'Haver grabbed my elbow and sharply yanked upward. I heard a tearing sound as pain radiated into my neck and down my shoulder blade. "Sit down right now," she said through clenched teeth and shoved me back into my seat.

I cried quietly. I used my fingers to add pressure to the socket of my shoulder. It ached like no other pain I had ever felt. I whimpered but could feel the piercing scorn of Mrs. O'Haver's glare. The fear she instilled in me was so paralyzing, I knew I couldn't ask for help.

My class stood and I obediently followed the line up to the stage. We were beginning the show. I stood in the crowd of mice whimpering and holding my shoulder, looking around at my classmates, who were stumbling through the song. Tears were streaming down my face. The lights were blinding me, so I couldn't see out to the audience. After an eternity, it was over. We turned, and marched toward the steps to exit the stage. My mother met me at the steps. As soon as I saw her, I felt safe to cry, and I let out a gigantic wail.

Mrs. O'Haver came running over.

"Shut your disrespectful little brat up right now!" Mrs. O'Haver snarled at my mother.

My mother picked me up into her arms, and I continued to wail, holding onto my shoulder.

"I saw it," my teenage sister came up behind us, pointing at the principal. "I saw her yank Kristy's arm really hard." In my short life I'd never seen anyone stand up to Mrs. O'Haver, and thought my sister was very brave.

"No," Mrs. O'Haver stood in my mother's path. "She has stage fright. This is ridiculous. She's ruining the show for the other students."

I was petrified of Mrs. O'Haver and quieted my wailing to whimpering. I still gripped my shoulder.

"She has to return to her seat," Mrs. O'Haver directed.

My mother placed me down on the ground, and the pain was so blinding, I stumbled backward, falling against my sister.

"No," my sister steadfastly said. "She's hurt. She needs to go to the hospital right now."

Then my dad approached the scene, trying to see what the commotion was about. My dad lifted me up, and I felt safe, towering over Mrs. O'Haver.

I was in an X-ray machine at the hospital,

then in a hospital bed. My dad had taken my sister and brother home, and was going to come right back as soon as he could. My mother spoke to the doctor.

"Nothing's broken," she said as she sat down on the side of the hospital bed. "You tore some ligaments. I'm sure Mrs. O'Haver didn't mean to do it."

Upon returning to school, I felt so vulnerable. I didn't understand why my mother forced me to go back. I was so young, and became so depressed. I spent my days sketching dark scenes in a sketch book. I withdrew from my friends, and refused to participate during gym or recess. During math class I would sink low into my chair, desperate not to call attention to myself.

17

Ski Vacation

"Get the ski poles you want out of the closet downstairs," my dad poked his head into my bedroom.

I was drowsy but excited because I knew we were going on an adventure to Vermont to ski. My parents had been talking about the trip for weeks. My dad had been working really hard and needed this vacation.

I pulled my quilt back and swung my feet around. I lay on my stomach and held onto the sheet so I could lower myself to the floor, because my bed was too high off the ground. I came into the kitchen and my mother was packing a cooler. She didn't notice me. She lifted the cooler onto her hip and walked out the front door.

Behind me, I heard the toilet flush. My brother came out in his feety pajamas and smiled as he walked past me. I used the bathroom, then returned to the empty kitchen. I figured everyone must be in the basement. I went down the spiral stairs to stand near the wood-burning stove. My sister was carrying my skis and my brother's skis on one shoulder, and her skis on her other shoulder. I sat next to the wood-burning stove to pet our cat, Princess. I felt sad that we were leaving her for the holiday, but she was curled up on a blanket sleeping, and I knew she'd be okay for a couple of days until we came home.

"Kristy," my sister said. "Get in the car."

I stood up and stuffed my feet into boots that were warm from the fire. I pulled on my puffy winter jacket and walked through the basement into the storm room and out to the driveway. It had been half-shoveled and packed snow crunched beneath my feet.

I climbed into the back of our purple minivan. Like all of the road trips we had taken before, my parents laid the seats down and piled up pillows and blankets, so that we could sleep during the drive. My sister took the front passenger seat. My dad was driving, and my mother was lying between me and my brother. My parents used a battery-powered combination TV/VCR to keep my brother and I occupied on long drives. I chose *The Lion King* for our first movie, and we settled next to our mother, both falling asleep to the opening song.

Two hours later my brother and I woke up. We stopped at a gas station and my mother and sister carried us inside to use the bathroom. When we got back in the car, my brother chose *Aladdin*. My father pulled back onto the highway. As the movie was ending, I started to think, *The cooler is taking up a lot of space in the back. The ski boots are next to the cooler. The skis are under the seat. The luggage is in the luggage carrier on top of the car…*

"Dad, where are the ski poles?" I asked.

"I got mine!" my dad proudly proclaimed!

"What? You didn't get our poles?" my sister gasped.

"I told each of you to pick out the poles you wanted," he said, laughing.

"What are we going to do without poles?" my brother asked.

"It's okay," my sister spoke over my dad's emphatic laughing. "He'll be laughing real hard when we get up there and he has to rent poles for all of us."

When I was young my parents told me we put up Christmas lights to make it easier for Santa to spot the houses that needed presents.

They said even if people don't put lights on the outside of their houses, Santa can still see the lights on the Christmas trees inside.

We took our vacation during Christmas, and stayed in a hotel on the mountain. I became very concerned that Santa wouldn't be able to find us in the hotel room. We didn't have lights or a Christmas tree. I voiced my concern, and my dad and sister sprung into action.

They went into the lobby of the hotel. A few minutes later they knocked on our door. When I opened it, I laughed. They stole a gigantic fake tree from the lobby, put it on a luggage cart, and brought it up to our room. The tree wasn't a Christmas tree, just a regular tree with waxy, fake leaves. They wheeled it into the room and unloaded it near the window. My dad took the luggage cart back to the lobby. My sister looked around the room and spotted a basket full of colorful yarn. She unraveled the yarn and used it to decorate the tree. She also hung socks and underwear from the branches. I thought, *This is the best Christmas tree we've ever had.*

I went to sleep hoping Santa would see our tree in the window, even though it didn't have any lights on it. When I woke up in the morning, I was elated! There were a couple of small presents under the tree and a big beautiful note on the tree. The note was from Santa and said that the rest of our presents were under our Christmas tree at home.

My family had been skiing for two days, and we were having so much fun. The slopes were perfect. Our last night there, it briefly rained, and then the temperature plummeted. The snow had become ice within a few hours. In the morning my parents decided we'd stay on easy trails and get a couple more hours of skiing in before we headed home.

"Cut across the slope, Kristy," my mother called out to me.

I pointed my skis, bent my knees, and pushed off. We took a wrong turn and ended up on a slope that was too steep for my brother and me. Our mother was leading us down the mountain. When I reached her, I looked back at my brother. He slid safely next to me. We looked up the mountain. My dad was halfway down the slope, and my sister was coming toward him. My dad spotted an out-of-control snowboarder barreling toward my sister. My sister slipped on ice and came tumbling down the mountain. In that same moment, in an effort to protect my sister, my dad cut across the mountain and collided with the snowboarder, who missed my sister by inches. My dad and the snowboarder became tangled and tumbled down the mountain, repeatedly slamming into the ice. When they skidded to a halt, the snowboarder popped up as if nothing had happened and sped away. My dad didn't get up. My sister, who was able to regain control, rushed over to him.

"Mom!" she shouted, "Go get ski patrol."

My mother told my brother and me to stay where we were. She turned and took off.

When ski patrol arrived, they lifted my dad onto a plastic, orange toboggan. My sister skied over to my brother and me. Heroically, she took my brother's skis off. She had him stand on the back of her skis, and she lifted me onto her back. Very slowly, she made her way down the mountain carrying both of us.

When we arrived at the snow-patrol lodge, our mother gave my sister the car keys, and told us to get dinner, then go wait in the car. A long time later we finally saw my mother and dad making their way toward the car. My dad was on crutches. My dad got in the passenger's seat, and my mother started driving. They told us my dad broke his knee and would need surgery when we got home to New Jersey.

18

What's Going On?

I woke up in the middle of the night. There was talking and footsteps, and the light in the bathroom was on. I stood in the door frame, and my mother was frantically digging through the cabinet, pulling out different medications.

"What's going on, Mom?" I asked.

She looked at me, "Everything's okay, Kristy, just go back to bed."

I complied. I lay back down, wondering who was in our house so late at night. I had school the next day, and I quickly fell back asleep.

In the morning my mother woke me up. "Daddy got very sick last night and is in the hospital now. He's going to be okay, and we're going to see him this afternoon as soon as you get done with school."

Sick? Alarmed, I asked, "Why can't we go see him now?"

"He needs to rest. I promise he'll be okay,"

my mother assured me.

I was on the bus, and my brother was next to me. The bus hit a pothole as we passed the hospital. I pressed my index finger to the glass and turned to my brother. "Daddy's in there," I explained.

We were in the hallway of the hospital, and my mother was standing at the nurses' station. A nurse said, "Children are not allowed in the ICU."

I thought, *Maybe this woman doesn't realize how much I love my dad.* My mother negotiated with the nurse, and finally she agreed that we could visit for twenty minutes.

We were next to his bed and he was smiling at us. He showed us the pulse monitor that was clipped to his finger. He was giggling to himself. He said, "they don't like me. All night I kept taking the pulse monitor off my finger, and it would make an alarm sound, and they'd run in here thinking I flatlined."

Hahaha! I thought. *My dad is so funny. He's always joking, and always doing something to get a rise out of people. He'll never die.*

My dad was home and standing in the kitchen. My parents told us my dad now had type-two diabetes.

My father began to explain, "I was working a lot, and it was so hot out. I kept drinking Snapple. For hours I was inhaling one Snapple after another. I couldn't get enough. I figured I was dehydrated. I should have been drinking water, but I also felt like I needed sugar."

My dad sat down at the table with a little black case. He unzipped it, and there was a beige pen and a square monitor inside. My dad took it out, touched the pen to his finger, pressed a button, and there was a loud click. When my dad pulled the pen away, a tiny bubble of blood pooled on his fingertip. He unwrapped a little test strip, put it in the monitor, and wiped his finger on the strip.

"Will I get diabetes?" I asked.

"As long as you stay healthy and don't get fat, you won't get it," my dad assured me.

The monitor beeped and I looked down. There were numbers blinking, but I didn't know what they meant.

"We're going to start eating a lot healthier," my dad said in a very confident tone.

My dad was sitting at the kitchen table with a plastic measuring cup. There was a large plastic tub with the lid screwed off, and my dad was scooping green powder out. I thought it was drugs.

"We're going to start eating this," my dad said.

"What is it?" I felt uneasy.

"It's healthy," my dad said. "You mix it into juice and put it in pasta sauce."

No way, I thought.

The green powder turned out to be completely disgusting, and even in pasta sauce I could still taste it. That led to very defiant mealtimes for my sister, brother, and me.

On another night my parents called my brother, sister, and me into the kitchen for dinner. We sat down and there was this cylinder-shaped thing in front of us. I knew immediately that I wasn't going to eat it. I had no idea what it was, but it had spinach, asparagus, and other vegetables wrapped in some type of meat, and tied together with butcher's string.

"Aunt Cathy's husband has type-one diabetes," my dad explained to us, "and he was able to beat the disease by eating very healthy."

The strict eating rules only lasted a week. My parents finally gave in, and we went back to eating normal food, which mainly centered around pizza, fried chicken, and ice cream. I did not understand the seriousness of diabetes. I was very relieved that our food became edible again.

19

Bastards

My brother, Charley, who was seven year old, was sitting in the front seat with the seat belt across his lap, and the shoulder restraint tucked behind his back.

I crawled around on the back seat of the car unrestrained.

I heard a thump, and the car jerked. I was thrown against the window and my head smacked the glass. I quickly sat down and fastened my seatbelt around my waist and shoulder. I sat up straight and braced myself by holding the handle on the door and pressing my feet against the back of the passenger's seat.

"Bastards!" my grandma stuck her head out the window and swerved into oncoming traffic. "You're all a bunch of bastards!"

My brother looked back at me, and the moment we made eye contact, we both heaved in laughter. We had no idea we were in physical danger.

The car continued to swerve, and my grandma veered off into the parking lot of a hotel, and came to an abrupt halt.

"Bastards!" Charley shouted, mimicking our grandmother's drunken rage. I laughed. She lifted her hand and smacked Charley in the head.

Abruptly, the laughter stopped, and my brother began to cry. Charley pressed his hand to where he had been struck. I felt really bad for him and felt rage toward my grandmother.

"Straighten up, or you're not going to eat tonight," she told us.

My brother and I undid our seatbelts and got out of the car. Our grandmother opened the trunk and pulled out a large plastic bag, which she stuffed into a large purse. My brother and I joined hands and trumped across the parking lot into a hotel. We followed our grandmother through the lobby and into a restaurant. We'd been to the restaurant before. Once a week they had an all-you-can-eat lobster buffet special. The hostess peered over her lectern disapprovingly at my brother and me.

"One adult and two children under the age of five," my grandmother said.

The woman looked down at us one more time. I tried to look away, hoping she wouldn't ask my age, which was eight years old.

"Okay," the hostess said with a huff. "Follow me please."

In the mostly empty restaurant, we were seated in the center of the room, close to the buffet area. I looked around at the booths on the outskirts of the restaurant, which had several couples midway through their meals. My grandmother instructed us to each take a plate and put two lobsters on them and come back to the table. As we were coming back, with our lobsters, a waiter approached the table.

"Would you like to place your drink orders?" The waiter asked.

"We'll just have water," My grandmother said.

He left, and we began eating. My brother and I cracked open lobsters with precision that most under-five-year-old children couldn't possibly possess. As we began eating, my grandmother took each of our second lobsters, then took Ziplock bags out of her purse. She slipped the lobsters under the table and they seemingly disappeared under the tablecloth. When we finished, our grandmother instructed us to go back, get a new plate, and get two more lobsters each.

When we came back, our grandmother was drinking a glass of wine from a paper cup. I sarcastically thought, *Oh boy! This is exactly what we need right now.* I also noticed that upon our return, our waiter was pointing toward our table and speaking to the hostess.

We ate our lobsters and, again, our grandmother took our second lobsters. We repeated this process two more times. Each time, I felt like more and more of the restaurant employees were staring at us. After all of us ate four lobsters each, and my grandmother had slipped twelve lobsters under the table, she said it was time to go.

When we stood up, our waiter approached the table and asked if he could get us anything else.

"No," my grandmother drunkenly hiccuped as she hoisted her gigantic old-lady purse over her shoulder.

She stumbled toward the hostess' station to pay the bill, which totaled $37 for one adult, because children under five ate for free, and we only drank water. The hostess asked to see inside my grandmother's purse. As the hostess reached out to snatch the purse off my grandmother's shoulder, my grandmother stumbled backward. The waiter came rushing toward the hostess with an empty box of wine.

"I found this under their table," the waiter said angrily.

"I don't have to take this abuse!" my grandmother exclaimed. She turned and stomped toward the door. My brother and I ran after her.

The hostess and waiter trailed after us, shouting that they were calling the police.

Quickly we pulled away from the hotel. On the street we swerved twice. Finally, we were back in the parking lot of our grandmother's assisted-living facility. We followed her as she stumbled back into the building.

In her apartment, Charley and I sat on the couch. She filled a red Solo cup up from the box of wine sitting on her kitchen counter, then held the wall until she got to her bedroom. Our grandma closed the door.

"Are you okay?" I asked Charley.

"Yeah," he assured me. "Let's just call Mom."

I got up from the couch and dialed our mother's phone number. "Mom?" I spoke into the receiver. "Can you come get us?"

She asked, "What's wrong?"

I said, "I don't know. Grandma's drunk and she hit Charley."

"I'll be right there," she said as she hung up the phone.

20

Blue Whistle Pops

I was in the passenger's seat with McNuggets on my lap, a soda squeezed between my legs, and a plastic Happy Meal toy by my feet. My dad was speeding down a dark road when red and blue lights flashed in all the mirrors.

"Aww, fuck," my dad said. He looked in the rearview mirror as he slowed down to the side of the road. My dad looked over at me, then looked in the side-view mirror to see the officer's car light come on. "Kristy," he said to me as he parked and the cruiser pulled up behind us. "I want to you chew up some of your food and spit it onto your lap."

"What? Why?" I asked.

"Right now," he demanded.

So I did it. I stuffed three McNuggets in my mouth and spat them onto my lap.

My dad smiled, then looked over to see the officer walking alongside our car with his flashlight out.

"Look sad," my dad said.

That wasn't difficult because I had a wad of spitty, gross McNuggets in my lap.

My dad put both his hands on the steering wheel, then when the officer was next to the window and his flashlight was blinding me, my dad took one hand off and rolled the window down.

"Do you have any idea how fast you were going?" the officer asked in his official voice.

"I'm sorry, officer. My kid threw up," he said as he leaned back so the officer could get a clear view of my chewed-up-McNugget-covered lap.

The officer peered into the car, looking at my face.

I looked scared, because I thought he knew we were lying. Then he pulled his head back and said, "Okay, get her home safe, which means drive the speed limit."

I felt a sigh of relief.

"Yes, sir," my dad confirmed. He rolled up the window.

As the officer walked away, my dad looked over at me and, in his most approving voice, said, "You did great, Kristy. You can have anything you want."

My dad's approval meant the world to me. Sometimes my dad would bring me this special candy from the city. It was a lollypop shaped like a whistle. I said, "I'd like a blue whistle pop, please."

"You got it," my dad smiled as we drove away.

A couple days later, I was happy, whistling around the house with my blue whistle pop.

"Kristy," my dad came into my room, "Do you remember when you helped me get out of that ticket?"

I nodded my head yes.

"I need your help again. I got a ticket for throwing a cigarette butt out of the car window on my way home from work yesterday. I need you to come to court with me and tell the prosecutor that I don't smoke because you are allergic, and that the police officer must have made a mistake."

"But that's a lie, Dad. You do smoke," I said.

"The ticket was for $250. Think about how unfair that is, that I should have to pay $250 for a tiny little cigarette butt," my dad reasoned with me.

I agreed with him, and a couple weeks later, I was sitting in a court room next to my dad. Knowing very little about the justice system, I thought I would have to go up on the stand, and I was really nervous. But then someone led us into a back room, where I sat at a table across from an old, thin, bald man in a gray suit.

"I'm very allergic to cigarettes and my daddy hasn't smoked since the day I was born," I lied to the prosecutor.

"You're a very good girl, and I can tell you love your daddy very much. Make sure he buys you something special for coming in to talk to me today. What would you like him to buy you?" the prosecutor asked me.

I thought about it for a moment. A smile stretched across my cheeks. "A blue whistle pop."

The prosecutor looked at my father and nodded, and then my dad and I were on our way home.

"Good," my dad said when we were in the car. "I love you."

I smiled, knowing my father was satisfied with my performance.

21

Secret

I looked up at my glass jar with a red plastic lid, and back toward my dad standing in the doorway of my bedroom. For every birthday, Christmas, Easter, and Halloween my grandma, aunts, and family friends would give me cards with money. Sometimes it was a five-dollar bill, sometimes a twenty-dollar bill. That money always went straight into my glass jar with the red plastic lid, and sat above my TV.

My dad had found a black 1988 Toyota MR2. He used to have a red one a long time ago but it had been stolen. Now he was asking me to help him purchase the one he'd found. He promised that when I was old enough, it would be my car, and that he would pay me back as soon as possible. I handed over my jar, which contained about $650, completely trusting my dad.

"Don't tell your mother," my dad winked at me.

I went to sleep that night feeling really anxious. *Why didn't my dad want my mother to know about the car? Aren't grownups always supposed to talk about big purchases?*

"Mom," my nine-year-old voice cracked in the privacy of her bedroom. "Dad told me not to tell you, but I feel like what he's about to do is a big deal and I should tell you."

The look on my mother's face was a familiar look of dread; my dad was capable of extremely erratic behavior. She swallowed hard, braced herself, and said, "Go ahead, tell me what it is."

I felt really guilty about telling her my dad's secret, but felt like something bad might happen if I didn't tell her. "Dad's going to buy a new car," I said.

She appeared relieved, then flustered. "Oh, boy, okay, thank you for telling me. You did the right thing."

A week later, it was in our driveway. A sporty, older, boxy race car. My dad was really happy, and in the end, I don't think my mother was really that upset he'd bought it. For a couple weeks I waited for my dad to pay me back, but it never happened. In my mind, I decided not to ask him about it, and instead to consider it my payment toward him for my martial arts lessons and ski passes, and all the other nice things he did for me.

22

Three One

Green Day guitar rifts drifted through the air of a warm summer night in New Jersey. Charcoal smoldered. Marinated chicken breasts sizzled on the grill. Emma and I were standing on the deck near the swimming pool. My sister's teenage friends were sipping beer in the hot tub. On the upper-level deck, my mother sat on my dad's lap at the patio table. My parents, laid back and happy, were entertaining our neighbor Mindy and her husband, Emma's mom, and some of my parents' other friends. We were having a party for my sister's sweet sixteen. She'd invited friends from her Catholic high school, and others who attended public school. But my sister hadn't arrived yet.

"Kristen and Emma!" my mother called from the upper deck. She was holding two paper plates.

Emma and I followed my mother into the house, and sat at the kitchen table.

"It's getting late now, girls. I want you to eat dinner, then put something on TV and chill out," my mother instructed.

"But we wanted to go swimming!" I whined.

"You'll have to wait until tomorrow. It's late. Eat, and don't come back outside," my mother said firmly as she closed the sliding screen door.

Emma and I had plans to watch our favorite TV shows, *Boy Meets World* and *Sabrina the Teenage Witch*. After finishing dinner we changed into our pajamas and went in the living room where we pulled blankets off the arms of the couch and started our first show.

As the show was coming to an end, I started feeling around.

"What's wrong?" Emma asked.

"Blanky, I forgot her outside." I felt uneasy.

Rolling her eyes Emma said, "Don't you think you're getting too old to have a baby blanket?"

"Mind your own business," I said sharply as I stood and stepped away from the couch.

"Your mom said not to go back outside," Emma warned.

I walked through the kitchen and pressed my face against the sliding glass door. More people swarmed both the upper and lower decks. My parents weren't sitting at the patio table anymore. I pulled the glass door open and walked across the upper deck. I stopped at the railing for a moment to devise a path through the herd of drunk teenagers. When I felt like I had a plan, I descended the steps into the crowd. I pushed my way through, being careful not to get knocked over. I was only half the height of my sister's friends, and I understood that alcohol distorts your perception. At the edge of the deck, I realized my parents were sitting at a table in the grass, which was the table I'd left my blanky under. I didn't want to get in trouble, so I quickly hopped off the deck and crawled on my hands and knees until I was under the table. I was careful not to bump into any of the feet that were tucked underneath. I spotted my blanky, snatched it off the wet grass, and stuffed it into my mouth. *Success!* I thought. I swiftly reverted and wiggled out from under the table. I climbed back onto the deck and began pushing my way through the crowd again.

And then this...person...This pale, gangly person in all black was standing in my way, and when I tried to step around him, he side-stepped to continued blocking me. I froze in fear and evaluated what he was wearing, which was in contrast to everyone else wearing bathing suits or shorts with light, colorful summer tops. The boys at my sister's party had short, neat haircuts that were buzzed on the sides, and the girls wore ponytails with bright scrunchies.

And then there was this menacing creature. He was wearing baggy black pants made of a heavy material and a black t-shirt with the Black Sabbath logo on it. He had chains hanging from his pockets and the insides of his arms were covered in weird black-and-blue bruises with weird red dots in the middle of each discoloration. When I looked up into his face, I became paralyzed with fear. He had a long black, curly, greasy mop for hair. It hung in his face, and he peered down at me with a predatory, vengeful stare like a demon.

"Three One, what's up, man?" Emma's older brother, Otto, cut in.

'Three One'? What kind of name is that? I thought to myself.

Three One glared at Otto, then reached back and grabbed a metal bowl filled with Nacho Cheese Doritos. Three One flung the bowl into the swimming pool. I watched as the shiny metal bowl sunk into the water, and the Doritos became soggy, and the orange cheese dissolved into the water.

"What the fuck, man?" Otto shouted over the music.

A group of people stopped laughing, halted their conversations, and turned to see what was happening. Quickly, as the attention grew, the tension mounted.

"Fuck you!" Three One shouted, then took a big step forward and shoved Otto backward, causing him to stumble back, but he was caught by the crowd that had formed behind them. Three One whipped around and snatched up a Super Soaker water gun, aimed at me, pulled the pump, and dowsed me with high-pressured, cold, chlorinated water. I immediately started crying. One of my sister's friends hoisted me into the air right as my dad stepped past me. In one swift motion my dad's powerful arm reached out and grabbed Three One by the hair. As my dad stomped across the deck, the crowd parted, and my dad dragged Three One out to the driveway.

My sister's friend put me down and I bolted up to the living room, and went straight to the front door.

"Emma!" I shrieked.

"What happened?" She came to meet me at the door.

"Look!" I pointed out to the end of the driveway.

Emma stood next to me and we watched two shadowy figures. One was massive, the other was nothing. A crowd of my sister's friends lined up on the lawn to watch. The massive shadow pummeled the puny shadow.

In his most masculine roar, my dad shouted, "Come on my property again, I'll drown you in your own blood. Touch my car, and I'll beat you until your mother can't recognize you."

After that, the crowd trickled back into the backyard. Emma and I looked at each other, and I swallowed hard.

"I'll be right back, then I'll tell you what happened." I said. I turned and went in my bedroom to change my soaked pajamas. When I returned to the living room, I told Emma everything, and then we watched the remainder of *Sabrina the Teenage Witch*. At the end of the show, we went to the front door. Three One was sitting alone in the dark, hunched over in the middle of the street. It was eerie.

"You think he'll do anything?" Emma asked.

"No," I said confidently. "My dad would kill him."

Emma and I put on a movie. We heard the sound of my father's MR2 start and got up to run to the door. The engine revved. The car rolled out of the driveway, then stopped for a moment next to Three One. My father said something to him, and a moment later my dad sped away.

"Weird," I said to Emma. We laid back down.

We got up one more time to look out the front door. Three One was gone, and so was the MR2. We laid back down and fell asleep.

The next day when we woke up, Emma's mom and older brother were sitting at the kitchen table, which was weird because they never slept over and only lived a couple streets away.

"Kristen," Emma's mom informed me. "Your parents are at the hospital. Your sister got in a car accident last night when she was on her way to the party. She'll be okay, and they'll be home in a couple hours."

Many years later I learned that, a few weeks after that party, Three One was arrested at a local motel for raping a seven year old girl.

23

Don't Ever Come Back

My kind teacher from second grade, Mrs. Wellington, was reassigned to teach fifth grade. Over the summer I was elated to learn she would be my teacher again.

One day, Mrs. O'Haver stood one of my classmates in front of the blackboard and told her to complete a long-division equation. The child trembled as the chalk slid across the board. I could see her mouth wording a silent prayer to Jesus. She was shaking, and her anxiety overtook her. She forgot to carry a number.

Mrs. O'Haver sneered as she spun the girl to face the classroom. Mrs. O'Haver lifted her open right palm and smacked the girl across the face, striking her to the ground. The girl let out a howl, and the rest of us snapped straight up in our chairs, shocked by what we just saw.

Mrs. Wellington ran to the girl and covered her with her body. Mrs. Wellington helped the girl up and told a boy toward the back of the room to get the nurse and an ice pack.

"Don't!" Mrs. O'Haver shouted. The boy froze as Mrs. O'Haver charged him, gripping a pointing stick. Heroically, Mrs. Wellington wrestled Mrs. O'Haver out of the room and into the hallway. Secretaries from the main office came barreling toward the commotion. One of them was the boy's mom. When she saw her son frozen, standing at the back of the room, she rushed in.

"Are you okay?" she asked as she pulled his head into her chest.

He pushed away and pointed to the girl who had been struck.

"Hold on, baby," she said as she left the room. A moment later she returned with the nurse, who quickly wrapped an ice pack in a hand towel, pressed it against the girl's face, and cradled her, lifting her up and whisking her out of the room.

The next day we had a substitute teacher who taught all our subjects, including math. The girl who had been struck was already back in class.

Two weeks went by. Our substitute teacher was okay, but we didn't love her the way we loved Mrs. Wellington.

My class was on the playground in front of the school. We all wondered where Mrs. Wellington had gone when, miraculously, she appeared across the parking lot. A group of girls swarmed her.

"We missed you!"

"Welcome back!"

"Where have you been?" Different innocent, high-pitched voices squealed and gleamed around her.

I stood back and realized she was crying. Without saying anything to us, but hanging her head low, she made her way into the building.

When she returned, she was carrying a brown cardboard box, a beige manila folder, and two picture frames. Her tears were heavier. She set the box down on the pavement and opened her arms. Two by two, she hugged each of us.

"I'm so sorry," she wept. "I have to leave now."

I watched her lift her belongings, hang her head, and walk into the parking lot.

I didn't understand why she would leave us. She was the best teacher I had ever had.

Several more weeks went by. We were approaching the end of the school year. I was standing in a small group on the playground. One boy was talking about going on vacation in Jamaica.

Another boy said, "You have to be really careful in Jamaica. I went there once. You have to stay on the resort. If you go out into the city, the Jamaicans will attack you."

Without much thought I recalled something my dad had said a couple nights before and just blurted it out, "Yeah, the darker you are, the dumber you are."

I was in the principal's office and she was screaming at me, and I was crying. I didn't understand what I had done wrong. Suddenly my grandma was there.

"You touch my granddaughter, I'll kill you," my grandmother said.

The principal reached out to grab me. My grandma cocked back and punched Mrs. O'Haver square in the jaw. She doubled back and fell over her desk. My grandma grabbed me by the wrist and dragged me down the hallway, and I waited as she stormed into my brother's classroom.

My brother came out of the room holding his backpack and his coat. We could hear our grandma shouting in the classroom. She stomped out, and we followed her out to her car, and she took us home.

The next day my mother was sitting in the front yard with me. She was gardening, and I was standing in the grass.

"Am I in trouble?" I asked.

"No, you and Charley are just going to start summer vacation two weeks early. Next year you'll go to a new school," my mother told me.

"A new school? Why?" I implored.

"You got expelled. But it wasn't your fault. The principal was a lunatic," my mother assured me.

In my entire life I had never felt such a tremendous sense of relief. I was so grateful that I wouldn't have to go back to that school. Nothing about the entire situation felt like punishment.

24

My Mom's Friends

For me, the summer between fifth grade and sixth grade was a season of solace. My parents agreed to send me and my brother to public school. I was really excited about going to the same school as Emma and was looking forward to not having to wear a uniform or pray in school anymore. There was one other private Catholic school in our county. I wondered why my parents didn't decide to send us there, but didn't want to risk them entertaining that thought, so I decided to stay quiet and enjoy the summer.

My parents liked to party. Every summer was full of house parties, long days in the pool, and long nights in the hot tub. My parents loved to entertain. We frequently had house guests who came to stay for a couple nights from the city. Some of my parent's friends were great, and I really looked forward to seeing them. Some of them were polite to me and my brother, but weren't "kid people", and I felt indifferent about them.

My mother had friends named Cat and Brandi. They were lesbians whom my mother was friends with from her previous job in the city. Brandi had a teenage daughter, and they would come from Queens to our house in New Jersey to spend weekends with us. I always liked when they'd come because they were a lot of fun.

My parents, Cat, and Brandi were on our deck getting drunk. I was standing in the hallway. A fight erupted and I froze as everyone barreled over each other, spilling into the kitchen. I watched my father's tremendous frame hoist Brandi by the waist of her jeans. She was struggling to get free, and Cat was trying to pry my father's grip. Everyone was stumbling through the house toward the front door.

My sister grabbed me and my brother and slammed my bedroom door shut, turning the lock. We sat on my bed listening to the fight.

We heard commotion near the front door and ran to my bedroom window to watch as my father tossed Brandi off the six steps of our concrete stoop and onto the front lawn.

The fight continued on our lawn, but my sister instructed my brother and me to sit on my bed. She was trying to keep us from watching them. I sat and thought about how lucky we were that my bedroom's door was intact and had a lock on it, and we were safe as long as we stayed put.

Several weeks before that night, my sister, who was eight years older than me, had a boy over and had closed her bedroom door. My father slammed his fists on the door and demanded that my sister open it immediately. She didn't. My father took one step backward, and with one swift, forceful front kick, he kicked my sister's bedroom door off the hinges. My sister's bedroom now didn't have a door, and my father refused to get her a new one.

When the fight was over, my sister said, "Stay in here until I tell you to come out." She got up, went into the hallway, and shut the door behind her.

My brother and I looked out the window. Cat was helping Brandi up, and they were stumbling toward their car.

"What the fuck is wrong with you?" I heard my sister scream. We heard some muffled talking.

My sister came back in my room and said, "We're going to have a sleep over in here tonight." She turned toward my TV, grabbed a Disney movie, and we all settled into my bed.

That summer something about the parties my parents threw changed. A lot more of them ended in fights. Fewer of my parents' friends that I liked came over. Our house guests were replaced by more of the ones I felt indifferent about. I kept myself occupied with the excitement of starting public school soon.

25

Public School

I was sitting in my classroom among an eager crowd of sixth graders. It was the first day, and I was elated to be there—in normal clothes. Not having to wear a school uniform made me feel pretty and, for the first time, made me confident in how I looked. I was finally free from the horror of Catholic school. While I appreciated the sacrifices my parents made to afford Catholic school, I was confident that I would be much happier in public school. In large part my confidence was because I had the same lunch period as Emma, who'd been my best friend since before kindergarten, and I believed our bond as best friends would be unbreakable in the sea of uncertain middle schoolers.

A teacher approached the door to my classroom. As programmed from Catholic school, I stood and said, "Good morning." I looked around. None of my classmates stood up. I looked toward the teacher in the doorway. She looked surprised. I looked at my teacher, who sat behind his desk.

"Are you okay?" he asked.

I suddenly realized they don't do that in public school. I sat down again. "I'm sorry, I didn't kn—"

The teacher in the doorway interrupted me, "It's okay, I thought it was sweet."

In Catholic school, I would have been seriously reprimanded if I didn't politely greet and address every adult.

During my first couple weeks in public school, I realized even more differences from Catholic school. The students received significantly less homework. Easily, I was the top student in my class, and sometimes asked for extra assignments on topics I was very interested in. I quickly realized the education I received in Catholic school was drastically better than the education the children in public school were getting. Regardless, I was so happy to be there.

During lunch time I sat with Emma and her friends, and, at first, it was easy to fit in. They liked me because I was doing so well in class. I was considered a "preppy" kid, and I relished in the role of being smarter and more disciplined than my peers.

One day I was in class and someone passed me a note.

It read, "Someone likes you."

Before I knew it I was dating a very nice boy named Hal. He was my first boyfriend. We didn't kiss, and rarely even held hands. He was nice, innocent, funny, and cute. He lived in the same community as me, though I didn't know him before sixth grade, because I attended a different school. One day he came home with me and met my dad. It felt important. My dad shook his hand, and then we went downstairs to play video games.

I was so happy. My teachers loved me. I was doing really well in every single subject. I participated in chorus, and on the track team. I still attended martial arts, and in the winter I was skiing. I was making friends and felt very accepted in my new school.

26

Roland

It was really exciting! Apparently, my dad had a long-lost brother named Roland, and he was coming to visit us for Thanksgiving. Roland had been given up for adoption when he was a baby, many years before my dad was born. My grandmother was nervous and excited to see the child she said goodbye to when she was only a teenager. They paid for a limousine to pick up Roland from the airport and bring him to our house. My mother told me that Roland was a truck driver and lived in Oklahoma. Oklahoma seemed like another world, and I tried to imagine what it would be like to live there. I imagined it was a desert—with vast open space. I imagined cowboys, tumbleweeds, spurs on boots, and horses. What I imagined seemed wholesome, western, old, and rustic.

When Roland arrived, I was surprised. He didn't look anything like my dad. He was older, balding, with gray hair. I soon disliked him.

He seemed rude, uneducated, brash, and confrontational. Over the next couple days, my dad and Roland spent a lot of time out of the house. My mother seemed irritable. I didn't understand what the problem was.

One night my dad came home. He was drunk, and he had a bandage on his shin. He was sitting in the living room quietly arguing with my mother. She eventually went to bed. I came into the living room and my dad told me to sit down. He removed the bandage. There was a bloody mess underneath. My dad had gotten a tattoo. He said it was for me and my brother, but it was so bloody that I couldn't make out what it was supposed to be.

After Roland left, my parents continued to argue. My dad was acting really weird. He wasn't going to work, and he was drinking all the time. I wanted them to stop fighting.

One night I was sitting on the carpet in my bedroom. I laid out my beloved CDs to admire them. There were the Backstreet Boys, NSYNC, 98 Degrees, Britney Spears, the Spice Girls, Savage Garden, and Christina Aguilera. I could hear my parents arguing down the hallway. I turned to my boombox and turned up the volume to drown out the yelling.

I heard my dad stumbling down the hallway. He fell over, into my door, and came crashing down onto my CDs. My mother came in to help him up and get him into bed. I started crying. My CDs were ruined. My mother came back in and apologized to me, and told me my dad was sick. I knew he wasn't sick. My sadness turned into anger. I plotted revenge, and that night when my parents went to bed, I went into the living room. I collected bottles of alcohol from the china cabinet and, one by one, poured them down the kitchen sink. There were two bottles I couldn't open. I felt frustrated, because I wanted them all gone. I remember knowing I would be in trouble, and knowing what I was doing was wrong. But I had a sense that this would help my dad.

I was starting to understand that my dad had a problem, and I needed him to stop. I wanted him to be healthy. I began realizing that all the arguments he was having over the summer with all our family friends were only happening when he was very drunk. The arguments he was having with my mother were when he was drunk. I just wanted him to stop.

When I was done dumping all the alcohol, I went to bed.

I didn't get in trouble. I don't remember my parents getting mad at me at all. I only remember my mother telling me a couple days later that I dumped $2,000 worth of liquor down the drain. She said my dad was extremely depressed because after Roland left, they realized he'd stolen about $5,000 worth of my mother's jewelry. My dad was really hurt because he'd thought Roland would become part of our family.

I felt like $5,000 was a fair price never to have to see Roland again.

27

Hello?

My sister had been away at college and was finally home for Christmas. Our entire family was coming to our house to celebrate. My dad erected the tallest and most beautiful Christmas tree I had ever seen. I was sitting in the living room. All the lights in the house were off, except the twinkly ones on the tree. Everyone except me had gone to bed. It was well past midnight. I was watching the lights illuminate the golden ornaments.

Startlingly, the front door swung open. Bells jingled. In her boisterous smoker's voice, Aunt Beth, my mother's sister, called out, "Hello?"

The dog started barking.

I was so startled that I couldn't speak.

Aunt Beth kicked snow off her shoes and stomped into the house. She took two heavy steps inside before my mother scurried in, "Shut up!" my mother said to her sister.

"Where's Stefanie?" my aunt was so excited to see my sister.

"Everyone's sleeping. The guest room is set up for you. Come in and go to sleep," my mother said sternly. "Charles is going to kick your ass if you don't shut up."

I was surprised to hear my mother say that about my dad. *But*, I thought, *he had been getting in a lot more fights in the past couple of months*. I really wanted to have a nice Christmas.

I was feeling anxious because it was 1999. There were a lot of news stories saying that on New Year's, Y2K would happen. I didn't understand exactly what the news stories meant, but I was under the impression that the world might come to an end, or that everything would blow up. It seemed important to me that that we cherish this Christmas, just in case it was our last.

Between Christmas and New Year's, Emma slept over one night. We were in my living room watching *Sabrina the Teenage Witch*. We idolized her and hoped to grow up to be as pretty as she was. We talked about her outfits, how she wore her hair, and what kind of makeup she was wearing. During our show, my dad came in.

Out of nowhere he said, "You know, Emma, you're getting really fat."

I was mortified. *Why would he say something so mean?* Emma wasn't fat at all!

Emma began crying, and I did my best to calm her down. She decided to call her mom and go home. I felt really bad, embarrassed, and angry at my dad. I knew, in the end, that he must have been drunk again. I went to bed that night hating alcohol, and blaming it for all my problems.

On New Year's Eve my mother put her foot down. We weren't going to have any house guests. We were just going to have dinner together and watch the ball drop on TV. I think my mother was feeling anxious about the small possibility of the Y2K news stories coming true.

My sister, brother, mother, my dad, and I were gathered in the living room. We were watching everyone freeze in Times Square. They looked happy and were cheering. I felt a little bit nervous.

"Dad," I started, "what if something bad happens?"

"Don't be stupid your whole life. Nothing bad is going to happen," he snorted meanly.

I realized he was drunk. I got up to walk away and thought, *Something bad is already happening.* I went to my bedroom, locked the door, and cried myself to sleep. My dad had never said something mean to me before. In our family, we were always praised for being intelligent, and for being gifted students. Intelligence was probably our most important measure of worth, and I was devastated that my dad had told me not to be stupid.

28

Hindsight

In Language Arts, which was my favorite subject, we were given an assignment to write about who our hero was. We had a discussion in class about what qualifies someone as a hero. Names like Betsy Ross, Elvis, and John F. Kennedy were brought up. I thought about who I wanted to write about, but decided to think it over for a day before I made a decision. Our teacher said we should choose someone who was strong, brave, and left a positive impact on the world.

That night I was in my bedroom, thinking of who I wanted to write about.

"Kristen, Charley, come in here," my dad called out from the kitchen. It was 8:30 p.m. and we had school the next day. "I want to talk to you."

My brother and I took seats at the kitchen table. My dad looked deep into our eyes. We were his eleven-year-old precious, little girl and his smart, tough ten-year-old son. His hand was tightly wrapped around a short glass with ice and brown liquor in it.

My dad began to tell us the story of his life. "I was born in Manhattan and lived with Aunt Cathy and Grandma in a small apartment. My dad was never really around."

"Why?" I implored.

"He had a wife and other children. They were my brothers, but they were a lot older than me," my dad told us.

It sort of startled me. I knew, without really knowing, that people sometimes have children out of wedlock, but that was something that happened far away. That didn't happen in my family. I thought about my grandma, and how much I loved her. I thought about the silk flowers she gave me, and sleepovers at her apartment, and cakes she helped me bake. It never occurred to me to wonder why I didn't have a grandpa.

"Where are your brothers now?" I asked.

"Well, you know about Roland. But he had a different father. My father's other sons' names are Joe and Paul. Paul is a kung-fu master. You would like him a lot. But both of them live very far away. They live different lives."

I thought about the martial-arts classes my dad, brother, and I took together, and how cool it would be to be related to a master.

"Grandma worked all the time, trying to make ends meet. Aunt Cathy and I never saw her. We were only two and three years old, and Grandma would leave us home alone all day. Sometimes Grandma would bring men home late at night, and they would beat me if I asked for food. When I turned four, and Aunt Cathy was five, Grandma had another baby. She told Aunt Cathy to take care of the baby. Aunt Cathy was barely old enough to dress herself, let alone care for an infant. She did her best. We worked together, making bottles and dressing the baby. One day Grandma came home, took the baby out of Aunt Cathy's arms and said, 'Okay, say bye-bye to the baby,' then sold the baby to a man named Carmine for $10,000. The very next day Aunt Cathy was sent to live with our aunt and uncle in Brooklyn."

I could see the devastation in my dad's eyes as he relived the pain of saying goodbye to his sister.

"I would open the refrigerator, and there would be nothing but a jar of mayonnaise, so I would sit there, all day, eating mayonnaise, waiting for Grandma to come home."

I really didn't understand what he was telling me. I had never experienced hunger, monotony, or abandonment like he was describing.

"My dad was really sick when I was growing up. Sometimes I would go to his house, but it was always scary, and I never felt welcome. He had diabetes and cancer from working in the Brooklyn Navy Yard, where the ships were filled with asbestos. My father would look me in the eyes and plead with me to hit him over the head with a hammer, begging me to kill him and end the pain. I was so scared. I never did it."

I imagined this man, my grandfather, talking to his son like that. My dad was kind and gentle. My grandfather pressuring his innocent son into killing him—it was unthinkable!

"My dad passed away when I was twenty years old. Aunt Cathy had to plan his funeral on her twenty-first birthday. I felt so bad for her, having to spend her birthday like that. My father had a savings account. There wasn't a lot of money, but he left it to Aunt Cathy, and told her to do what she felt was right with the money. Aunt Cathy decided to split it evenly four ways. Joe was livid. He felt that, as the oldest son, he should have been left all of the money. That's why we don't see him or your Uncle Paul."

My dad got up from the table and poured himself another glass of brown liquor.

"Where I grew up, things were really tough. One day when I was twelve, I was outside playing in the schoolyard with my friends. Twelve-foot fences surrounded the playground, but this older kid climbed the fence. He was going around with a big black belt buckle and told children to give him their lunch money. When he turned to me, I told him he was crazy. So he started swinging the belt buckle around and hit me in the back of the head. I pressed my hand to the back of my head and felt a large cut with blood gushing out. Without thinking I lunged toward the kid and tackled him to the ground. I grabbed him by his ears and slammed his face into the pavement over and over until one of his ears fell off in my hand."

My dad wasn't bragging, only recounting. I didn't understand why he was telling us these stories, but I always loved hearing him talk.

"By the time I was eight, I was riding the subway by myself every day to go see Aunt Cathy in Brooklyn. On the subway platform, I met a girl one day. She was the most beautiful person I had ever seen. A few days later I went to see Aunt Cathy and I was stunned to see Aunt Cathy playing with the beautiful girl I met in the subway. It turned out that the girl was her neighbor. I knew instantly that she was going to be my girl."

My dad turned and smiled toward the living room, where my mother was watching television.

"The first time I seriously proposed to your mom, I was eleven years old. We were always together. We broke up only one time, when we were sixteen. Your mom dated a guy named Richard. I dated a girl named Charlene. A few weeks later, I was on a date with Charlene, and we bumped into Mom and Richard. That same night, your mom and I got back together, and Charlene and Richard got together. Years later, Charlene and Richard ended up getting married."

I wondered what Charlene and Richard were like and hated the idea of my parents not being together.

"By the time I got to high school, I only had to take shop and gym class. I had already completed math and my other subjects. So at night I would drive a cab. I saw everything: drugs, prostitution, you name it. A couple times I had prostitutes in the back of my cab, fucking or doing whatever to their customer. I would just keep my eyes on the road and turn the radio up."

I could tell my dad was questioning whether or not he should have told us that. It was a lot to take in. I knew what sex was, but I didn't know there was an immoral way of going about it. Instead of stopping, my dad pressed on.

"One night I was taking a break at a pub. I was watching this young kid bet on pinball games with some gangbangers. I was laughing because the kid lost all his money, hat, sneakers, and shirt. Finally he bet his pants. He didn't want to give them his pants, so he started running down the street, and the gang members started chasing him. I ran to the hair salon next door and told the kid's mother what has happening. She ran out of the salon with curlers and wires sticking out of her hair and chased them down the street. By the time she caught up to them, the police were arresting the gang members, because it's illegal to bet with a minor. The kid ended up getting his clothes and money back. I laughed as I watched the kid's mother drag him up the street by his ear. She smacked him a couple times, but I could tell it was out of love that she disciplined him."

My dad got up to pour another glass of the brown liquor. I liked the story about the betting kid.

"Another night I stopped to get a drink in a gas station. I was picking what I wanted when I heard someone say, 'Don't move or I'll fucking shoot you.' I thought it was one of my friends being stupid, so I turned around, and was taken back. There was a gun pointing directly in my face. The gunman was twitching, probably high. I took a step backwards, and again the gunman said, 'Move again and I'll blow your head off.' I jumped to kick the gun out of his hand. He pulled the trigger and shot me right above my knee. The pain was excruciating. After the shot, the gunman fled the building. A police officer arrived on the scene and took me to the hospital. I waited two hours for a nurse to come in and clean the wound. Finally, when she came, I pleaded with her for pain medication. She ignored me. I tried to deal with it. She was able to remove the bullet, and started cleaning the wound, but I couldn't take the pain anymore. I walked to a drug store, got an Ace bandage, and let it heal by itself."

My dad moved his leg out from under the table to show us the blue and purple indent where the bullet had entered his leg. I cringed at the pain he must have suffered.

"When I was twenty, I married your mother. We went to Disney World for our honeymoon. We rented a convertible to drive onto the beach, but I got it stuck in the sand. We had to call a tow truck. When we got home, we went to live in your mother's grandmother's basement apartment. Your mom worked in a bank and I went to college. We saved enough money to move into a two-bedroom apartment. We got pregnant with Stefanie. Your mom got a good job at the phone company, and a couple months later, she was able to get me hired too. We continued to save and dreamed of someday moving to Florida. We had friends who owned a large two-story house in New Jersey. They told us they needed money to finish renovations on the house. We talked about it and agreed that New Jersey would be safer and better for Stefanie. We decided to give our entire savings to our friends, and in exchange, we would move into the second floor of their house. They lied to us. They didn't tell us the house was in foreclosure. Shortly after moving in, we were forced to leave. We were devastated, flat broke, and had to provide Stefanie with a place to live. Against our better judgment we ended up going to stay in the basement of your mom's father and stepmother's house in Brooklyn. They were horribly mean to Stefanie, and we knew that situation had to be as brief as possible. Your mom's stepmother actually told Stefanie, who was only four-years-old, that she wasn't allowed to eat Grandma and Grandpa's food. We worked really hard and sacrificed for six months. We were able to save $8,000 and move into the house we live in now."

My dad paused to look around our home. He smiled. He got up again and poured another drink.

"A few years later, you were born," he looked at me and smiled. "And then you," he looked at my brother and smiled again. "I was so happy to have my family. I love you more than you could ever imagine. But things couldn't stay simple. Right before Kristen was supposed to start kindergarten, she got sick and was in the hospital. I was on my way to see you. I was with Stefanie and we got in a car accident. The car flipped, and I herniated two disks in my lower back. I lived with constant pain but couldn't afford to take time off from work for surgery, so I just lived with it. Then I developed sleep apnea. I couldn't sleep and it was driving me insane. I decided to have surgery to help with my breathing, but it went horribly wrong. That's when I had to start sleeping with the breathing machine. I started missing a lot of work. But there was one big job I did that summer, where I started drinking Snapple all the time. One night I went into a diabetic coma and was rushed to the ICU. I had to take even more time off from work, and I could tell the company was becoming very annoyed with my requests, even though they were legitimate medical emergencies. Around that time, I got called to jury duty. When I returned to my job at the phone company, they fired me. They said there was no record of my summons. I got a letter from the courthouse proving I had, in fact, served. They refused to reinstate my job. Your mother and I knew we had to fight to get my job back. We spent our entire life savings to hire a lawyer, who eventually even took my IRA. We borrowed against the house and exhausted every resource we had. In the end, we lost the court case because the lawyers never filed under the Americans with Disabilities Act, which was the real reason the phone company fired me. In the end, the judge awarded me only $3,000 and I wasn't able to get my job back. I got really depressed. I thought that if we went on a family ski trip, it would help me forget about all the problems at home. I broke my knee when that snowboarder crashed into me. That put me out of work for a couple of weeks, and we fell really far behind on all our bills."

My father looked at us. His eyes were glassy, and his skin was red.

I asked, "Why didn't Grandma take care of you better?"

He said, "I don't know, Kristen. You should ask her."

My mother called from the living room, "Kristen, Charley, it's late. You have to go to bed. School tomorrow."

My brother stood up and went into the bathroom. My dad poured another drink. He looked broken, exhausted, and depressed. I went to him and hugged him. My father whispered, "I'm in so much pain." I released him and looked deep into his brown eyes.

My mother said, "Kristen, bed."

I turned to walk down the hallway. I looked back and my father said, "The only thing everyone in the world has in common is that they feel alone."

I went to sleep.

He killed himself.

~after~

29

I Wasn't Ready

After my dad died, I missed a week of school. During that week I sat down to complete my assignment of who my hero was. When I sat at the keyboard, only one hero came to my mind. I thought about all of the sacrifices my dad had made to give me and my family a good life. I thought about all his suffering, both physical and mental. I thought about how, despite things being hard, he taught me how to ski, scuba dive, and do martial arts. My dad taught me how to be a good person, how to have self-respect, and how to persevere. I stayed up late that night, recalling everything he'd told me the night he died.

The next day I was sitting at the dining-room table. My dad's sister, Cathy, and mother's sister, Beth, were helping to set the table.

My mother asked me, "What do you think about going back to school tomorrow?"

What? So soon? I thought. "I'm not ready," I said firmly. I felt like my world had just changed so drastically. I still needed time to regain my bearings. In only a week I'd lost my father, spent several days at Emma's house, and had a funeral—I'd just gotten home. I wasn't ready to go back to school.

"Of course you'd say you're not ready," my mother said coldly. "But you have no choice. You're going back to school tomorrow."

When I entered homeroom, I was startled because my teacher presented me with a sympathy card that was signed by all my classmates. The general statement everyone made to me was that they were there for me if I needed to talk, and they were very sorry for my loss. I felt embarrassed and caught off-guard. I felt like it was my business to tell or not, but I also felt like I couldn't hold on to any anger because everyone was being so nice.

In Language Arts class, I handed in my paper. The following day the teacher asked if I wanted to read it in front of my class. I told her I'd read the first part, and she could read the second part. The first part graphically described finding my dad dead. The second part chronicled his life, tribulations, and triumphs. When I finished, I looked around, and nearly the entire class was crying. My teacher's face was red and streaming with hot tears, and she took me in her arms.

Over the next couple weeks, I spent more and more time staring out the window, crying, and completely ignoring my lessons and homework.

I was in history class. I had my face in my arms and unprompted, I began to weep. I couldn't stop. My teacher told me to go to the bathroom and put cold water on my face.

In the bathroom I continued to cry. I slid down against the wall, heaving and crying, missing my dad terribly.

Someone came in. "I'll go get someone," she said, running out the door.

The school psychologist came in. "I'm so sorry. How can I help you?"

"Emma," I said. "Can you go get Emma?"

"We can go find her together," the psychologist said as she helped me up.

I found out from another student that Emma was in the woodshop. I was in the doorframe, still crying. Emma was holding her project and wouldn't make eye contact with me. I was trying to explain that I was in a lot of pain, and really needed some time to talk to her.

"Mr. Smith won't give me more time to finish my project," she said and she turned away.

"Yes, he will," I insisted.

She walked away. The school psychologist ushered me into the hallway and helped me into her office. I stayed there and cried for a long time.

After that, Emma and all the girls who sat at our table, whom I'd thought were my friends, literally turned their backs on me. I wasn't welcome at their lunch table anymore, and was exiled to the far corner of the cafeteria.

In the hallway I heard whispers that I was weird. I heard rumors that I was going to be put in a mental institution. Fewer and fewer of my peers wanted to talk to me. They groaned when I was put on their team in gym class, and made excuses when I tried to find a new table to sit at in the cafeteria.

I couldn't stop crying. I completely gave up on schoolwork. I would sit in class and doodle until my pencil was dull. I was a zombie. I lost all of my friends. I broke up with Hal. My teachers were becoming visibly frustrated with me. The only time I ever opened my mouth was to talk about my dad.

Finally, in class, someone exasperatedly asked, "Why do you *always* talk about your dad? Don't you know he's dead?"

30

Family Cruise

"I'd really be happy if we just stayed home and had a party at the house," My sister said to my mother.

"Your dad would have wanted us to take a vacation. That's what we always did together, was vacation," my mother explained to her.

"But Mom," my sister tried to reason. "I could really use the money for college, and Kristy and Charley are going to need money for college. Or you could pay off a big chunk of the house."

"I have a plan to pay off the house. There will be plenty of money left over after this trip to pay for your education. Come on," my mother whined. "I really need a vacation after all this stress."

Reluctantly my sister said, "Okay, but let's choose a short trip to keep the cost low."

In April, it was my sister's birthday, and we were going on a cruise to celebrate. My sister was bringing two friends. My mother invited her sister, Beth, and her boyfriend of twenty years, my Uncle Andy. She also invited my father's sister, Cathy, and her husband, Uncle Jesse. After a lot of squabbling, Aunt Beth decided she couldn't afford to take off from work, but Uncle Andy was firm that he deserved a vacation, and this was a good opportunity. Uncle Jesse decided he wanted to save money to complete renovations on his house, but Aunt Cathy said there was no way she was going to miss her niece's birthday. My sister was going to stay in a cabin with her friends. My mother, brother, and I were going to stay in a cabin, but because only four people could fit in each cabin, Aunt Cathy and Uncle Andy were going to stay in a third cabin.

My brother and I found some children to play tag with, and late at night we were running across the deck of the top floor of the ship.

"Wait, look!" my brother grabbed my wrist and whispered.

I spun around as my brother pulled me behind a stack of lounge chairs: Aunt Cathy and Uncle Andy were making out behind a pile of deck chairs.

"Let's go tell Mom."

"Mom!" we said in unison as we caught up to her. She was inebriated at a bar, talking to a man with gray hair.

"What's wrong?" she asked us.

"We just saw Aunt Cathy and Uncle Andy making out!" we said with urgency.

Our mother hiccuped. "Just leave them alone."

My brother and I looked at each other as we walked away helplessly.

We didn't see Aunt Cathy or Uncle Andy the rest of the trip. We were disappointed on the night of my sister's birthday, which was the purpose of the trip, when they didn't come to dinner. At the end of dinner, my mother and sister were discussing their lack of attendance through clenched teeth.

We returned home from the trip very late at night. My sister had flown back to Florida for college.

"Go to bed," My mother instructed my exhausted brother and me.

As I walked toward my bedroom, Aunt Cathy sat at the kitchen table, holding Uncle Andy's hand. My mother sat down. I closed my bedroom door and fell asleep, hearing a long and muffled discussion.

Many years later I learned that Aunt Cathy and Uncle Andy had been having a secret affair for a very long time, but that my dad would have never allowed his sister to leave her husband for my mother's sister's boyfriend. I felt like they really betrayed my dad by waiting until after his death to publicly be together.

31

South Korea

A charity campaign was started at my martial arts school to help raise money so that my brother, mother, and I could attend a trip to South Korea, which was going to take place the summer after my dad died. Members of the school donated to help cover the costs of the trip. This trip would have been a dream-come-true for my dad, and because of the love, kindness, and generosity of fellow martial artists, we were able to join them.

We went with Grand Master Kwan, his wife, his daughter, and some of the students from our school to get our pictures taken for our passports. Grand Master Kwan took us to a Korean neighborhood and we had a meal at a Korean restaurant. My brother and I both ate chicken fingers.

We were on a plane for a long time. Finally we landed in Alaska. I pressed my face up against the cold glass in the airport. The sun was low in the sky, and I remember thinking that Alaska was really flat. I had imagined gigantic mountains, tons of snow, and at least one majestic moose. I was disappointed to find out we weren't allowed to leave the airport during the layover.

After 16 hours of travel, we finally arrived in South Korea. We were standing in the airport, waiting for our luggage to come off the plane. My brother and I watched a TV commercial where a Korean woman was magically shrunken down. Suddenly she was riding a giant bottle of dish soap around her kitchen, and laughing erratically.

We were in Seoul, and it was very crowded. I was told we were near a government building with important people inside. There were guards with gigantic automatic riffles strapped to their chests marching back and forth. My mother went to get Coca-Cola. A group of male police officers surrounded me and put their faces two inches away from mine. They stared into my green eyes. I was scared and tried to back away. One of them held me by both shoulders to keep me close. Grand Master Kwan was trying to talk to them in Korean. Finally they let me go and walked away. Grand Master Kwan said they had never seen anyone with green eyes, and wanted a close look. He said they weren't like the police in America, and you couldn't tell them to stop, or they would arrest you, and that I was lucky they left me alone.

We were at a beautiful hotel, which Grand Master Kwan booked because it had five stars. After checking in we realized we were the only guests in the hotel. There was one employee at the front desk, but no cleaning staff, valet, or restaurant workers. We went to our rooms and went to sleep. Early the next morning, there was shouting in Korean in the hallway, then someone banged on our door. It was Grand Master Kwan, yelling through the door to us that we had to leave the hotel immediately. My confusion smothered any fear. We got on our tour bus, and as we were pulling away, a thousand riot police wearing gas masks were marching toward the hotel with giant clear-plastic shields and batons. As we drove toward the road, I heard someone say the hotel employees were rioting.

On our third day, we left Seoul and went to a Buddhist temple in the mountains. We had been told it would take a couple hours. I took off my shoes and played a card game with another girl from my martial-arts school.

"My dad gave me these playing cards," she said, "so make sure you don't lose them."

Right as I opened my mouth to respond, there was a huge impact, and I was knocked off my seat. A second later, the ground was gone. I fell sideways and landed on one of my friends. Luggage spilled out of the overhead compartments and flew out from under seats. Glass shattered. The bus was skidding. Another impact, then compete stillness.

My hands were crushing the playing cards as though they would save me from any further danger. *Okay, I can probably let go now.*

I stood up and started looking around for my brother. He was unconscious, and immediately I feared he was dead. Before I could reach him, an adult lifted him up and carried him toward the front of the bus. There were two very young children in the back of the bus with me. I picked one up to carry her out.

Toward the front of the bus, I heard a loud *kiop* and a crashing sound. Someone told us to move forward. Barefoot and carrying a toddler on my back, I walked over broken glass and fallen luggage. I ducked down and shimmied out of the hole Grand Master Kwan had kicked through the windshield. When I got out, the child's father lifted her off my back, and I stood straight up. It was raining harder than I had ever seen.

I looked up a muddy slope, which was littered with bushes and boulders. It was steep but only about a six-foot climb. The other passengers and I used the bushes to pull ourselves up to the shoulder of the highway.

Someone told us to walk farther down the highway in case the bus exploded. Once we were far enough away, we just stood there in the rain while rubbernecking Koreans in their cars stared at us as they creeped by the accident. I looked up the highway to see our completely destroyed tour bus, which was hanging on its side over the guardrail, teetering toward a ravine.

An ambulance came and I was told to get in, along with a dozen others. We arrived at a filthy hospital. There were roaches, gnats, and clods of dirt in the corners. Many of the people we were traveling with had been very seriously injured—broken hands, broken ribs, concussions. They were lying on stretchers that appeared old and rusty.

We realized we couldn't find my brother. Grand Master Kwan spoke to police and hospital officials, who called around to other hospitals and found he had accidentally been taken to a different hospital but was in stable condition. Grand Master Kwan and my mother left to be with my brother.

A Korean news crew came in and they were filming us. They spoke in Korean and put their microphones in people's faces. We had no idea what they were saying and didn't want to speak to them anyway. Finally a group of men banded together and pushed them out of the room.

Later someone said the bus driver had been drunk on sake and had driven the bus onto the center divider of the highway, which was what had made it flip. Someone else said we had been skidding toward a cliff when a white car slammed into the back of the bus, causing the bus to change direction and come to a halt on the guardrail.

That night our entire group met in the lobby of our hotel. We were told that the most injured people were already on flights back to Alaska and would be getting surgery as soon as they landed. There was a discussion I tuned out of because it seemed very boring. The adults were mainly talking about lawsuits.

When we finally made it to the Buddhist temple, the entrance gates looked like a swastika. I was confused and asked about it. Our tour guide said the arms of the symbol face the opposite direction of the Nazi symbol, and this Buddhist symbol was a sign of peace.

Hitler stole the symbol and changed the direction of the arms to make it a sign of hate.

Inside the temple there was a bed of smooth river rocks stacked on top of each other. Some of the stacks were only four-rocks high. Some stacks were impressive, varying in the size of stones used, and several feet in height. There must have been three thousand stacks. We were told that this was a way to focus and live in the moment, and that the higher you could make your stack, the closer you got to self-actualization.

In another temple monks did a martial-arts demonstration for us. Their balance, precision, and accuracy were absolutely stunning. We watched one very old man do kicks and handstands and jump across wooden pillars—feats that should have been impossible at his age.

At another point we watched women walk into the forest with gigantic baskets on their backs.

Jokingly my mother said, "There they go, to gather our lunch."

When the women returned, they in fact brought our lunch—of leaves. Literally leaves they had pulled off trees.

I didn't eat that afternoon.

We went to the Kukkiwon, the World Taekwondo Headquarters, in Seoul. We watched incredible demonstrations by Korean taekwondo students. Because of the bus accident, Grand Master Kwan said we weren't required to compete, but I assured him I wanted to compete regardless. I only competed in sparring. I felt intimidated because no one spoke English, so I wasn't sure what the judges said to me. I fought three fights and destroyed each of my opponents. I was excited to know I was a talented martial artist, even on the other side of the world.

One day we went to a restaurant. We were all supposed to eat the same thing: a soup with octopus tentacles sticking out of it. There was no way I was going to eat that. I said I had to go to the bathroom. My mother said she would come with me. The owner led us downstairs and through the kitchen to the bathroom. There was a stream of dirty water running from the bathroom to a drain in the kitchen floor, through a pile of unrefrigerated eggs. There were flies and roaches crawling on uncovered food. My mother and I went into the bathroom—a small room with a porcelain hole in the ground. We took turns squatting over it and laughed about how unusual it was.

Finally we were on the plane home. The three of us sat together in a row and my brother was hyper, ignoring my mother's orders to calm down and be still. He spun around and knocked a bottle of orange juice on me. My mother didn't have any extra clothes in the carry-on luggage, so I spent the sixteen-hour plane ride covered in orange juice.

32

Charter School

In the summer between sixth and seventh grade, a review of my academic performance was conducted. Administrators at my school noticed that I was at the top of my class in the beginning of the year in sixth grade, but after my dad's death, my grades had plunged. In a meeting with my mother, they told her they knew I didn't have a learning disability. My teachers were concerned with how disconnected I had become and noticed I didn't engage with the children they thought were my friends. They decided to send me to an experimental charter school, which focused on technology. I was told the school had much smaller class sizes and more advanced lessons, which they thought I might enjoy.

I felt like going to a new school was the fresh start I needed. I didn't think I could ever repair the friendships I had lost. I hoped that charter school would have all of the good aspects of Catholic school and none of the bad. I couldn't wait for the summer to be over, I was so excited for the change.

When school finally started in the fall, I was so happy. I quickly made friends and felt accepted. I got the impression that my teachers enjoyed having me in class. I loved the complexity of the assignments and the heavy workload. I felt like I was being given college-level work, even though I was only in seventh grade. We were learning advanced mathematics, how to build robots, and to use complicated computer programs.

One day I was sitting in the waiting area of the principal's office. I don't remember why I was there—I wasn't in trouble. The principal's door was cracked open, and I could see inside. I saw him French kiss my Language Arts teacher.

Innocent and naïve, I truly didn't know what I was looking at. I turned to the secretary and said, "Aww, that's cute!"

She very sharply sneered, "Mr. McKulla is happily married."

I was startled that she responded like that. I was momentarily confused. I assumed she meant the principal and the Language Arts teacher were married to each other. I didn't know any better. I walked out of the office and didn't think about the incident for the rest of the day.

The following day I arrived at school, eager to learn. Upon entering the building, I felt like the principal was grimacing at me as I stepped off the bus. I had an uneasy feeling but went to my first class anyway.

Approximately a half-hour later, an announcement came over the loudspeaker, instructing me to report to the main office. I compiled. When I arrived, I was surprised to see my mother sitting there.

"What did you do?" my mother asked me.

"Nothing." I was genuinely confused. I couldn't recall any recent instance where I had caused any problems.

My mother and I entered the principal's office. My Language Arts teacher was seated in the far corner of the room. The principal held up several pieces of paper, which I suddenly recognized to be a report I had turned in a week ago on Amerigo Vespucci. The principal claimed that I had plagiarized sections of the report. He said it was punishable in the court of law and carried jail time.

"I didn't," I stammered to explain. "I was just listing the facts I found on the internet." I thought I had correctly cited all my sources and put quotations around each fact I used.

The principal persisted, stating that the school didn't tolerate plagiarism and had decided to expel me.

I was devastated. Attending that school was the best thing that had happened to me in such a long time. When my dad had died, I lost all my friends and sense of self in my last school. Charter school had become a place I felt I could flourish in.

My mother tried to argue in my defense. She offered several solutions, but the principal refused to consider any of her suggestions. I left that day with my head hanging low. When I got in my mother's car, I fell asleep on the way home.

I was on the couch and woke up delirious.

"Kristy," my mother was shaking me awake. "You have to swallow these pills. Drink this milk and eat these pancakes."

I was in incredible pain. My neck felt stiff and my stomach felt raw. My mother lifted me and helped me sit upright. I swallowed the pills she'd given me without asking what they were.

She asked, "Do you remember going to the doctor yesterday?"

"What?" I questioned. Pain shot through my temples. "No, I don't remember."

"Incredible. You've been unconscious for four days. Yesterday our neighbor carried you into the car, and we took you to the pediatrician. The doctor did a full exam on you, but you didn't move one time. You don't remember that?" she implored.

"No, not at all," I shrugged. I felt extremely drowsy and irritable. My eyes started closing on their own. My mother shook me again.

"The doctor said he's never seen anything like it. Eat all of the pancakes, and try to stay awake," she finished.

I ate two more bites of the pancakes, sank into the couch, and fell back asleep.

The next day I woke up with a pulsing migraine. My mother said she was going to take me to see a psychologist in the afternoon. She cooked lunch for me, then helped me get up from the couch. My legs were dragging under me. They felt like they weren't connected to my body. My mother hoisted me on her hip. I tried to fight the exhaustion and focus on forcing my legs to cooperate. We stumbled to the kitchen table, where I sat and took more pills. I kept trying to put my head down and nap for a minute longer, but each time my mother shouted in my ear, shaking me and forcing pasta into my mouth. Despite all her efforts, my eyes kept involuntarily closing. After about a half-hour, the pills I had taken started to work. I felt a little more awake, and my migraine subsided. I still felt weakness in my legs, but was awake enough to walk, unsteadily, to the car.

The psychologist seemed nice. He asked me how I was feeling about school, my dad, and my friends. He asked what I wanted to be when I grew up, if I played any sports, and what my relationship with my family was like. At the end of the session, he asked if I wanted to come back and talk to him again, and I said yes. Upon leaving he spoke to my mother in the lobby.

On the way home from the session, my mother told me I would be going back to public school the next day. I felt indifferent about it and angry that I didn't have a say in how I was going to live my life.

When I returned to public school, they decided to take me out of advanced-placement classes and put me in regular classes. I was relieved because my former friends who had previously ditched me were in advanced classes, and I didn't want to have to face them.

The regular classes felt remedial. I befriended some of the bad kids who sat in the back of the classroom and never did their homework. I refused to participate in class and spent most of my time trying to fit myself into the bad kids' conversations.

In the last couple days of seventh grade, I was invited to a party by three girls named Carissa, Lily, and Lindsay. I hoped it would be an opportunity to solidify a new group of friends.

33

The Rock

For the first couple days of summer, I argued with my mother a lot, so I stayed in my room. She was acting irritable and tense. I couldn't understand what she was so angry about, so I ignored her.

A few days later was the party I'd been invited to. I called Carissa and she gave me the address.

She lived close enough that I didn't have to ask my mother to drive me. I walked to Carissa's house and knocked on the front door.

I was surprised when the door opened. A plume of smoke wafted out, and a guy who was at least ten years older than me answered. I was nervous and assumed I had gone to the wrong house.

"Get in here and close the door," I heard Carissa's voice demand.

I slid inside. I was relieved to see Carissa, Lily, Lindsay, and a few other familiar classmates. Carissa introduced me to everyone. Most were Carissa's sister's high-school friends. The last person I was introduced to was Carissa's dad. I shook his hand, then took a place on the couch.

"You want a hit?" an older guy asked me as he was pushing a weird glass tube in my face.

"No, thanks, I'm good." I said as I passed the glass thing to the next person. I gathered from the conversation in the room that they were smoking marijuana out of a bong—the glass thing. I was fascinated that they were doing drugs with their dad. I wanted to seem cool, but didn't want to do any drugs, so I tried to stay out of the conversation.

After a half-hour of awkwardly avoiding the bong and socialization, Carissa took Lily, Lindsay, and me into her room. We spent several hours listening to Blink-182, putting on makeup, and talking about people from school. They asked me for dirt on all the preppy kids from the advanced-placement classes. I felt no loyalty to those people who had abandoned me, so I told them everything I knew. Anything that came up that I didn't have an answer for, I made up. When I realized they liked the stories

I made up, I concocted even more cynical things to say. Their giggling fueled my exaggerations and fabrications.

When it got late, I walked home alone. I felt really optimistic about these new friends.

The next day Carissa called and told me to meet her, Lily, and Lindsay at a place called "the rock." I imagined it was a restaurant or something. I didn't have any money at all and was really nervous that they'd think I was a loser for not being able to buy something. Carissa gave me directions. I scavenged around my house and was able to scrape together two dollars in change. I hoped it'd be enough to at least buy soda. I set out walking, not having any idea what to expect. When I arrived, I laughed, because it was literally a big rock. Kids were skateboarding around it, smoking weed, and listening to music. It was butted up against a wooded area. Some kids were hiking into the woods, and there was a big group sitting on the rock around a boom box.

We spent all summer at the rock. We'd stay out until the sun came up, hanging out with high-school kids. We talked about our families. Each of us had a very different home life. Carissa's mother left when she was seven, and her dad was always high. Carissa's teenage sister was the parent in the house. Lily's older brother was in prison. She had four sisters. One was older than her, and the rest were younger. Her dad was always away on business trips. Her mom worked the afternoon shift at a restaurant, so they rarely saw each other. Lindsay's parents lived together but slept in separate rooms. She had a thirty-year-old sister who had no plans of ever moving out of her parents' house. By the end of the summer, I felt like I'd gotten to know Carissa, Lily, and Lindsay really well, and felt lucky to have new friends. Our families were different, but each one had different aspects of dysfunction that made me feel really connected to those girls.

Carissa, Lily, and Lindsay shared their clothes and makeup with me. I started developing an inappropriate sense of style for my age: I hiked up skirts that were already too short and figured out how to turn a bandana into a tube top. I painted my eyelids black, and someone gave me a goth spike bracelet, which I thought was very cool.

I spent most of my time out of my house. For a couple of weeks, I rarely saw my mother. When I was home, I ate cereal in my bedroom and tried to learn all of Eminem's lyrics.

One night, I was on AOL Instant Messenger while finishing my dinner of Lucky Charms. As far as I knew, my mother hadn't come home in three days. My brother and I kept ourselves occupied. For hours into the night, I stayed on AOL and my brother played video games. My brother was the more responsible of the two of us and would usually finish his game and go to sleep around midnight. I would stay awake all night, until the sun came up, getting lost in AOL chat rooms. I was addicted to the attention I got for being pretty. I also hoped to find someone who was living in a situation similar to mine to chat with.

"Kris," my brother peeked his head into the room. "Why isn't the cat moving?"

"What? Where is she?" I asked, looking up from the keyboard.

He led me out to the deck. Our cat we had had our whole lives was stretched out on the deck, contorted with an extreme arch in her back, not moving at all.

"Princess!" I called to her. "Pss, pss, pss, Princess!"

She didn't move.

"Let's call Stefanie," I said to my brother. I went in the kitchen to dial the phone.

"Hello?" my sister in Florida answered.

"Hi, Stef, I have some bad news," I said.

"What is it?" She sounded nervous.

"Princess. She's not moving. She's on the deck, stretched out in a really weird way. I think she's dead," I told her.

"Where's Mom?" she asked.

"I don't know. She hasn't been home in a couple of days. What should I do?" I asked.

"Get a towel out of the bathroom and lay it over her body, then go back inside and leave her alone. Don't touch her," my sister instructed me.

"Okay, thanks," I said and hung up. I turned to Charley and said, "Don't go back outside. I'll take care of it."

I went in the bathroom to retrieve a towel, then returned to the deck. I laid the towel over our cat. I was suddenly struck with terror at the dark night in the mountains and hurried back inside. Instead of going back to the computer, I went in the living room. My brother was on the carpet in front of the big TV and had already started another game.

"Hey, Charley, let's watch a movie," I suggested.

Immediately my brother turned off the video-game console. He turned and smiled at me. I liked that I could make him happy with my company. By that time in our childhood he and I weren't spending very much time together. I was always out of the house with my friends or buried in the internet. He was always playing video games.

"I'll pick a movie. You go make popcorn," my brother said as he sprang up and went down the spiral staircase.

I went in the kitchen and popped the popcorn. When I came back in the living room, my brother had the tape on pause. I sat down and smiled, because I knew exactly what we were doing. Since tiny children, my brother and I would play this game where one of us would secretly choose one of the hundred Disney movies we owned while the other one would make a snack. Then we'd press play and the one who had made the snack had to guess, based on the previews, which movie the other one picked.

My brother and I sat on the couch my dad had died on. Watching that old Disney movie was familiar and comforting. We both fell asleep on the couch. When we woke up, I hoped the cat had miraculously risen in the night. I went out to the deck. I was shocked; she was gone! But upon closer inspection, I found the towel neatly folded on the patio table. I called my sister.

"Stefanie?" I started.

"Yeah?"

"The cat is gone off the—"

"Yeah, I know. I asked the neighbor to come and get her so he could bury her," My sister explained.

"Oh," I pondered. "Okay, do you know when Mom is coming home?"

34

Goodbye, Taekwondo

After we returned from South Korea, my mother began helping Grand Master Kwan with office work at our martial-arts school. I assumed money was tight, and by helping him it decreased the cost of our lessons.

Leading up to testing for my black belt, I had been given the privilege and responsibility of the warm-up for children's classes. With Grand Master Kwan looking on, I had been trusted to lead the warm-ups for the past year. Now, with my new black belt, I felt comfortable doing it alone and had done so for the past few classes.

I stood at the front of the class and called, "Attention!" Everyone fell in line.

Some of the children were approximately my age, but most were younger. With my black belt I felt really proud. I had earned the position to lead and teach and hopefully make the children in Grand Master Kwan's school more focused and respectful. Those, I thought, were the two most important attributes to becoming a successful martial artist.

Grand Master Kwan and my mother were in the office with the door shut. I assumed he would come out to take over teaching when I got closer to the end of the warm-up. But as I was completing the stretches, the office door did not open. I shrugged and led the students in their first lessons of the day: kicking and punching drills. I was happily surprised—class was going so well. The children were taking commands and striving to improve their accuracy. The other students seemed to trust my maturity and know I was knowledgeable about Taekwondo.

The office door still shut, I continued teaching forms, self-defense, and sparring technique. Soon there were only ten minutes left until class was over. I ordered the students to the back of the room, so I could organize an obstacle course.

The entrance to the school opened and I looked over. It was Grand Master Kwan's wife. I lifted my hand to smile and wave to her. She scowled at me and turned away. I wondered if she was angry with me or something else. I turned my attention back to the obstacle course.

Children were laughing and running wildly. Eventually I looked at the clock, and realized it was three minutes past when class was supposed to end. I directed the students to put the obstacle-course components away, then line up so we could bow out. The adult students were waiting for their turn to come on to the mat. I was about to open my mouth when I heard my mother speak.

"Kristy," she interjected as she came out of Grand Master Kwan's office.

I looked over at her, unsure why she was interrupting the class.

"We have to go." She stated.

I looked back at the class and asked the highest-ranking student to complete the bowing out ritual. I walked off the mat and felt like the adult students were staring at me. I slipped on my shoes and followed my mother out to the car.

"We're never coming back," my mother fumed.

"What, why?" I asked.

"Mrs. Kwan just accused me and her husband of fooling around behind her back. I would never. I can't believe she would say that. But that's how Korean women are. They're very jealous," she said very matter-of-factly.

35

Take Me Out to the Ball Game

Because we were no longer going to attend martial arts school, my mother decided we needed to get involved in another sport. Without giving me a choice, she signed me up for softball, and signed my brother up for baseball. I never had any interest in playing softball. My mother kept reiterating that it would be good for me to try new things and meet new people.

My mother was able to get the mother of another girl on my team to bring me to practice and the games. The girl was not friendly toward me, so I would sit in silence in the back of their minivan. Without any explanation from my mother as to why I had to participate, softball became a thing that I hated, that I did alone. My mother never came to my games, but never missed any of my brother's practices or games.

I envied the lady who volunteered to be my team's team mom. She was a thin, pretty woman with three happy children. Her daughter was my team's pitcher. She'd come to our games with big bowls of orange wedges and animal crackers. I'd always think, *Where the hell is my mother?*

Every game was the same. I was always the last to bat on the lineup, and I was always given two unbelievably boring innings to sit in the outfield and pick blades of grass. Other than that, I sat on the bench, ate snacks alone, and watched good, involved moms cheer for their daughters.

One day my brother's baseball coach, Evan, was at our house.

And then he was there more often.

And then he was there all the time.

And then his wife, Shelby, started coming over sometimes.

I didn't understand what was happening.

Pretty soon, Evan started coming over almost every night for dinner. And then he'd be there in the morning when I woke up for school. If my mother was home, Evan was there. Evan became this ominous, looming presence. I was relieved to go to school and put some distance between us. He was oddly controlling and my mother asked his opinion about everything.

36

Detective Work

"I don't think we should do this," my brother cautioned.

I didn't care. I used a butter knife to pick the lock of my mother's bedroom door. Once open, my brother and I entered. My mother had been out with Evan for about a week, and we were running low on food, and were completely out of lunch money. I didn't understand why she was acting so crazy and was hoping to find clues in her bedroom.

My brother combed through the mess on her dresser, and found several small piles of change, which he collected into his baseball cap.

I opened my mother's nightstand. Sitting on top of everything else was a red velvet box. I took it out and pressed the golden button to open it.

Inside, there were old pictures of people I didn't know, and a couple of handwritten letters. Carefully I opened one and began reading it. It was dated 1995 and was from my dad. The letter said he was doing his best to make it through rehab and come home to our family a better man. The letter apologized over and over, and thanked my mother for standing by him, despite his addiction.

I opened several more letters. Some were dated as far back as the '70s. Some would have been from the time my sister was a baby, and some were dated after the initial letter I had read. All of the letters swore *this* would be the last time. All of them thanked my mother and promised he would be a better man for her.

I heard a car pull into the driveway. Quickly I refolded the letters. My brother tried to put the change back on the dresser the way he'd found it. We replaced the box and hustled out of the room, shutting the door behind us.

We peered out the front door. It was Shelby. She came up the hill, then up the front steps, and let herself in through the front door. She was carrying a thin metal tray.

"I brought the two of you dinner," she said.

She went in the kitchen, turned the dial on the stove, and put the metal tray in the oven. She walked down the hallway but stopped before walking into my mother's room. Slowly, she opened the door, peeked her head around the corner, and paused. It seemed as if she was looking for someone. She grunted a frustrated noise, then turned back toward the kitchen. My brother and I stood near the kitchen table.

"Take that out of the oven in fifteen minutes," she instructed us.

"Okay, thank you, Shelby," my brother called to her as she marched out the front door.

I went to my room and lay down. I thought about the letters, and how it suddenly made sense that we would go on vacation, but my mother would tell us our dad couldn't come because he couldn't get off of work. I knew my dad had had a problem. I just never understood the magnitude of it.

I lay there and wondered where my mother was going all the time.

37
9/11

An announcement came on over the loudspeaker. "All eighth graders, please report to the gymnasium."

In unison, my classmates and I compliantly stood and walked together through the hallway, down the stairs, and into the gym. We were pleased with the unexpected break from class, and took our places on the bleachers, finding friends who were in other classes.

The principal called our attention, "Everyone, settle down."

I thought it was a strange way to start an unscheduled assembly. Then I realized there were tears in his eyes, and tears in the eyes of many of the teachers standing off to the sides.

"Just a little while ago," he cleared his throat, "the World Trade Center was attacked."

A buzz grew in the crowd and I heard someone ask, "What's The World Trade Center?"

I didn't know, so I didn't say anything. I assumed it was a building in Europe. Maybe it was where the United Nations met? I wasn't even sure what the United Nations was. My limited understanding was only that they were a group of representatives from every country in the world, who gathered to discuss world issues. It seemed like a logical conclusion to me that they must meet at a place called the World Trade Center, and that place would be located in Europe, since that's where most countries were concentrated.

We were sent back to class. Moments after taking our seats, the loudspeaker spoke again, "Amelia and Corey Campbell, come to the office. Your mother is here to bring you home."

My teacher picked up a piece of chalk and drew in a deep breath, when the loudspeaker interjected a second time, "Heather and Courtney Babcock, Michael Banks, Aaron Cooper, Melissa, Melinda, and Melanie Mayfield, please report to the office."

A teacher came in, took my teacher into the corner, and then they both went into the hallway. A third time, the loudspeaker crackled.

This time it called off twenty more names, instructing them all to come to the office.

The remainder of the day continued like that. Every couple of minutes there was another announcement with a long list of students being called down to the office to go home. *Why isn't my mom coming to get us?* I wondered.

As I moved from class to class, the number of students continued to dwindle. The entire day, nothing was taught. For long stretches of time my teachers would leave the classroom unattended and congregate in the teachers' lounge. When left unattended, the few remaining students were relatively well behaved. We understood that something really important had happened, but still hadn't pinpointed what it was, and had no idea that it was happening forty-five minutes from us.

At the end of the day, I met my brother in the bus line. I told him something really bad happened today, but I didn't know what it was. Then he told me, "My teacher kept the television on all day. New York City got attacked by terrorists. The whole city got blown up."

I was shocked. I was scared. Our aunt lived in New York City. I was afraid for her life.

When the bus brakes screeched us to a halt, my brother and I bolted off the bus and up the hill to our house. "Mom! Mom!" we shouted.

We burst through the front door.

I shrieked, "New York City got attacked today!"

"I know," she slurred nonchalantly, then robotically took a seat in the living room in front of the television that was playing harrowing footage of airplanes slamming into the towers. Her eyes were glassy and her pupils were huge. I realized she must be high.

"Is Aunt Cathy okay?" I asked.

"Yeah," my mother seemed uninterested in talking. "She's fine."

"Why didn't you come get us from school?" I asked.

"You were safer in school." she continued to slur.

I was disappointed by her answer. I knew she didn't care about me on a day-to-day basis, but I assumed a national tragedy and the onset of a potential war would encourage her to protect her children at least a little bit.

"Mooooooooooom!" my brother whined from the TV in the kitchen an hour later. "There aren't any cartoons on."

Sharply my mother shouted, "Shut the fuck up. The world is coming to an end."

I turned around to watch her swallow another fistful of painkillers with her big glass of wine.

Then she looked at me and said, "I'm glad your father is already dead, and wasn't alive to see this happen. He would have run into the buildings to save people. He would have died in there."

38

My Dream Come True

He's dead, he's dead, he's dead, he died, he's dead, he's gone.

The snow is outside. The storm was so bad. The power is out in the entire county. It's cold; nature stands still. The earth is mimicking his lifeless body because it hates me. The whole world and the whole universe hates me.

The ambulances and police cars line up on the street. The paramedics rush in to find his wife frantically counting compressions on his chest. One paramedic turns to usher his two young, distraught children out the door. They hold the rail, and descend the icy, unshoveled steps, followed by a police officer who warns them to be careful.

A plastic yellow board is carried in. Two police officers lift his wife on either side and she stumbles backward, gasping for air through her hysteria. The yellow board is placed on the area rug. Paramedics kneel down, surrounding him on all sides. With incredible precision they're getting into position, unzipping bags, and pulling out small machines and wires. One paramedic shouts, "Clear!" and the defibrillator jolts a shock to his heart. A mask is strapped to his face, and a paramedic begins squeezing the manual pump, pushing air into his chest. Again, "Clear!" and everyone momentarily backs away. One paramedic uses a stethoscope to listen to his heart. He looks up, grimly shaking his head side to side.

"Again," one of them orders.

Another jolt, and then they all continue protocol. His wife drops to her knees to pray to God. "Charles, don't leave me. Please, God, don't take him now!"

The yellow board is slid next to the man, and four of the paramedics hoist him onto the board. They crank straps to secure his body, and then with a heave and a grunt, they lift the man up, and carry him toward the front door.

His wife rises to her feet and rushes to their bedroom to put on the first shoes—his shoes—that she can find. She rushes out the front door. The ambulance is already pulling away. A police officer offers her a seat in the passenger's side of his vehicle and promises to follow right behind the ambulance. The sirens click on, and the wheels start rolling. She is ten feet behind the ambulance. She presses her head back against the seat and looks up at the rifle stored on the roof of the officer's car. She squeezes her eyes closed, and in her mind, she bargains with God. *God*, she prays, *don't do this to me. Don't take my husband. I can't do this alone.*

In the ambulance the paramedics continue to shock his body, but there is no response. They don't realize the youngest member, their volunteer, accidentally forgot to load new batteries into their equipment. The driver, so focused because of the poor road conditions, requests assistance navigating the streets, hoping they can make it to the hospital in time to save this man they've never met.

As they arrive, the paramedics push open the doors. Chaos ensues as they put the wheels of the stretcher down. Another call is coming in on the radio. They rush him up the ramp. The automatic double doors at the hospital aren't opening. They use their fingers to pry them open.

The officer, rushing to keep up with the ambulance, skids on the road. He apologizes over and over to the wife while guaranteeing they'll make it to the hospital safely. She continues to pray, over and over. In her mind she tells herself, *Our love story won't end like this. It can't. Charles, you're going to make it.* Finally, the police officer pulls up to the hospital. The ambulance is already gone. The officer's car is still rolling when she swings the car door open and rushes up the ramp into the emergency room.

Frantic, she shouts, "Charles DiBella, I'm Charles DiBella's wife! He was brought it by an ambulance a few minutes ago!"

"Yes," the receptionist says as she pushes back her rolling office chair. "Please come this way."

The receptionist leads his wife to double doors, waves her security badge in front of a box on the wall, then leads his wife to a waiting room. "Please sit right here. The doctors will come out for you soon."

In the examination rooms beyond the waiting room, doctors and nurses rush in every direction, tending to too many critical patients. They're understaffed; the storm was so bad that many of the hospital employees couldn't make it to their shifts on time.

Accidentally, a nurse, tired and overwhelmed, hangs the wrong clipboard on the bed of the wrong man. Doctors hurry around this man, shocking his chest and pumping air into his lungs, but the heart monitor flatlines eerily and stoically they accept that they lost this one. They hang their heads for a moment, then are reminded of all the other patients who need their attention.

The doctor, whose sleep-deprived mind is occupied with thinking of all his other patients, pulls the clipboard off the dead man's bed.

They move on.

It was a tremendous mistake. In the chaos, no one realized his paperwork had been misplaced.

Meanwhile, in the waiting room, his wife continues to plead with God until the horrific moment when the doctor, a stranger in a white coat, appears.

"Mrs. DiBella," the doctor looks bleak.

He doesn't even need to say it. She drops to her knees, sobbing uncontrollably. The doors burst open. Neighbors and family friends spot his wife on the ground. They surround her. She is shaking and her breathing is labored. They shush her and hold her tightly. She cries there for a long time.

"Let's try to stand up," someone says to her. "We're all going to help you. You are not alone."

Her friends and neighbors lift her to her feet. But it is all for nothing, because she stumbles and collapses back to the ground. She thinks to herself, *How could God do this? How much more pain can I withstand? Charles was everything to me, the rock which I stood on. My family can't be a family without him. I can't live without him.*

After some time, a representative from the hospital comes out to greet her. "Mrs. Di Bella, I am so sorry for your loss. We have some paperwork we need you to sign. Do you want the deceased to be cremated, or do you have burial plans?" The representative pushes a clipboard with papers in front of her. She isn't ready to see any of this in writing.

"I don't know, I don't know," she whimpers over and over.

A neighbor pushes the clipboard away, "She needs a couple minutes."

She stands up, then falls to her knees, and begins to seizure. The representative rushes through the double doors, and two nurses rush in. They clear everyone away from the wife, and moments later her seizing body is hoisted onto a stretcher and rushed into the emergency room. A neighbor follows close behind to answer questions about her medical history.

He wasn't the man who died, even though the form on the clipboard said so. His naked body lies on a cold metal table beneath a white sheet. He shifts, and his eyes open. Dim light flickers, masked by the white sheet completely covering his head. He realizes he doesn't know where he is. His hearing becomes extremely alert. Ice-cold sweat consumes him, and his anxiety overtakes his breathing.

He senses that he is alone and that, wherever he is, no one has been here before.

His fingers twitch. They pinch the sheet; slowly pulling it off his forehead, exposing his eyes.

He rolls his head to the side. His ear touches the cold metal of the table. His eyes dart back and forth. He's petrified. He's a massive, powerful man, but he feels like a child. He can hear a phone ring very far away. It goes unanswered.

In one clumsy motion he heaves his body up and off the table. His feet touch the ground and he falls to his knees. He realizes that aside from the sheet, he is nude. He looks up; the lights in the ceiling are dull yellow, flickering, powered by a generator. He grips the sheet, wraps it around his body. He brings his fingers to his forehead and squints his eyes. He has a debilitating migraine.

There's a faraway crash. Adrenaline catapults him to his feet. Stumbling and struggling and gripping the rails on the walls, he makes his way down the hall, clutching the sheet to his naked body. His breathing is panicked, his body sweating.

In a room to his left he sees slacks hung over a chair. He enters the room. There's a curtain hanging from the ceiling, pulled back enough to see an elderly man lying in a bed with his eyes closed. An elderly woman rests with her eyes closed in a chair by his side.

The elderly man moans.

He grabs the pants and bolts out of the room, hopping as he pulls the pants up. He approaches another man sleeping in the waiting room, stretched across a row of four chairs. The man's baby entertains itself in its stroller. He peers around a corner, checking to make sure no one is coming.

He creeps close. The baby stops, looks up, giggles. The sleeping man draws his knees to his chest.

He sees Nikes and a winter coat. He looks at the baby, motions to shush it. The baby laughs louder, extending its tiny arms to be picked up. The sleeping man groans, lifting his hand and pushing the stroller slightly.

He grabs the Nikes and the coat. Barefoot, he runs to the automatic door, but it does not open. He smacks up against the glass. The thud wakes the sleeping man.

He looks over his shoulder at the groggy sleeping man, who quickly realizes his belongings were just stolen. He panics, uses his fingers to pry open the automatic door, squeezes through the opening, and takes off.

The ice beneath his feet. The frigid air in his lungs. The headache made worse by the sun reflecting off the snow. His heart pounds against his naked chest. At the street he looks to his left.

The man who was sleeping runs out of the hospital and can be heard yelling, "He stole my wallet! He stole my shoes!"

He looks to his right, and struggles running barefoot through the snow. He is topless. He grips the shoes and the coat and sinks into three feet of snow. Despite the frigid cold, he sprints, getting farther from the hospital.

Five blocks away he is huffing. The air is too cold and it's burning his lungs. His skin is turning red and white. His feet are throbbing.

The adrenaline is wearing off and he's starting to feel the effects of the cold. He puts his arms into the coat. He puts on the sneakers. He pulls the hood over his head. His ears are burning. The legs of his pants are soaked.

He feels a lump in the back of his pants. He pulls out a brown leather wallet. The picture on the driver's license is a younger version of the old man sleeping in the hospital. Two Visas, a MasterCard, and an American Express. Twenty-seven dollars.

He crouches in a covering for a bus stop. He searches the pockets of the coat. Newports and a lighter. Seven cigarettes left. He pulls one out, lights it, inhales. It's warm and familiar. He holds it in his mouth. In the second pocket he finds another brown leather wallet. This one's license has the picture of the man who yelled at him as he was running out of the hospital. He turns the center flap. A picture of the man's family is tucked in the plastic display. A bus pass, library card, and some business cards fill the pockets. One debit card. Seventy-three dollars.

The bus is here. He gets on, swipes the bus pass. The driver looks through him. Another bum. He walks to the back of the bus, takes a seat next to the heater. He slips off the soaked shoes and puts his bare feet on the heater. The pants are dripping wet too.

He opens the second wallet and stares at the picture. He asks himself, *what the hell just happened?*

The bus stops. It lets on four more people. A Hispanic woman in a trench coat takes a seat in the back of the bus, near him.

She speaks, "I so jealous! Me granddaughter in Flor-e-da. Sun and palm trees. I here, cold and wet."

He looks at her. *Florida?*

He thinks for a moment, then confidently says, "That's where I'm going!" as if that had been his plan since he woke up that day.

He thinks to himself, *my family must be in Florida. I know I will find them there.* He knows he must have family—everyone does!—even though he can't remember anything about them. He can't even recall his own name.

He rides the bus the rest of the day. Eventually the pants dry and his feet become warm.

He makes several transfers, and after nearly seven hours he puts on his shoes and walks off the bus. From the station he hitchhikes south.

While catching rides he doesn't take off his shoes, because he has no socks. He doesn't take off his coat, because he has no shirt. He rides quietly, patiently, and focused. He is friendly and pleasant to those who give him rides. He listens to their stories. He acts as a psychologist or mentor to some. He avoids questions about himself, mostly because he doesn't know the answers. He just knows his family is in Florida and he has to find them.

In North Carolina he stands on the shoulder of I-95 with his thumb out. Cars and trucks speed past him. He tries to stand tall. He tries to appear harmless. It's still cold, but nowhere near as cold as it was in New Jersey. Finally a pick-up truck pulls over.

He sits in the passenger's seat, riding with a girl on her way back to college. Christmas break was hard for her. Her family doesn't understand her. Her boyfriend doesn't understand her. She's going to break up with him when she gets back to school. Alcohol, cigarettes, and pot understand her. This is her second year of college, and probably her last. She has better things to do. She's going to move to Los Angeles, start a new life, and become a famous singer. She drives, and she talks, and he listens. Five hours later, coming to the border of Georgia, she stops talking and looks over at him.

"Why don't you have any bags?" she asks.

He doesn't say anything.

"Why don't you take off your coat? It's getting warmer."

He responds, "I can't. I don't have a shirt."

"I need gas," she says as she flicks on her blinker and gets off at an exit.

He pulls out twenty dollars and gives it to her.

"Thanks."

She goes into the convenience store. He waits in the car. When she comes out, she carries a plastic bag. She gives him a plain black T-shirt.

"This was the only one big enough for you," she says.

"Thanks, I appreciate it."

While she pumps gas, he gets out of the truck to put on his new shirt. He's surprised by how warm and humid the air is.

She drops him off on a street corner in downtown Miami.

Over the next couple months, he finds work among illegal immigrants. He spends his days on the roofs of houses. He befriends Cubans and Mexicans. He finds a lot of work because he fluently speaks English, is strong, and intelligent. For reasons he can't explain, he has a lot of electrical knowledge, and is able to complete jobs, illegally, at a fraction of the cost other electricians would quote. Several contractors begin to use him regularly.

He spends his nights and rare days off walking the streets of the city. He doesn't know how to find his family and can't remember anything about them. Still, he is convinced that if he continues walking and looking, he will find them, or at least find clues to remind himself of what he's supposed to be looking for.

Many lonely months go by. No clues come.

Through friends, he meets a beautiful Cuban woman. She cleans houses for a living. She is kind and gentle. They fall deeply in love. He becomes protective of her. They have a modest wedding with traditional Cuban music and food. They live in an apartment in the very bad part of town with eight of her family members, each sleeping on mattresses, which line the walls in every room. He dreams of someday buying her a house.

They have a baby. She's a beautiful baby girl with curly brown hair and brown eyes and light brown skin. Her name is Carolina and they love her.

His desire to provide his wife and his daughter with a good, safe home grows.

He turns to a friend whom he's always known to be involved with drugs. He thinks to himself, *Sure, I can do it. I can sell for just a little while, save the cash, and give my family the life they deserve.* It all makes sense in his mind. He's earned the trust and respect of the illegal immigrant community, so selling drugs becomes a real option.

His first assignment: Dress as a tourist. Travel east toward the ocean. Enter the Holiday Inn, knock on the door, room 623. Take the luggage from the room. Find the white Honda Civic parked beside the hotel. Pull the hat down and wear sunglasses, avoid the view of the security cameras. Pretend to bend down to tie your shoe. Key will be under the driver's side rear tire. Put the luggage in the trunk. Get in the car and drive west. Drive four miles over the speed limit. Make sure to use blinkers, and come to complete stops at stop signs. Take the luggage to the Budget Inn, park in the back of the parking lot out of view of any surveillance cameras, find room 203. Knock, drop off the luggage, take public transportation home. Easy enough?

He's not nervous. He feels like he's done this before. He arrives at the Holiday Inn, finds room 623, knocks, and enters. A Jamaican is smoking a cigarette. A Hispanic girl sits on the bed looking at the floor, a bruise across her cheek.

The Jamaican sees him see her, gets agitated, and hurries him out of the room. He wheels the luggage behind himself, walking casually, pausing to breathe in the salty ocean air. He looks around. He blends in perfectly with the fathers who have their daughters on their shoulders. He thinks of his beautiful Carolina, and how he will take her on vacation some day.

In the parking lot, he tilts his hat down and walks in the sand to avoid the security camera. He finds the Honda Civic. He bends down to tie his shoe. He finds the key, stands up, unlocks the trunk, places the luggage in the back, and gets in the car.

Ignition. The car blows cool air as if it had just recently been driven. He looks in the rearview mirror and carefully pulls out of the spot and exits the parking lot.

Drive four miles over the speed limit. Turns on the radio. Lights a cigarette. He looks up. A police car is driving behind him. He turns off the radio, begins to get nervous.

Fuck!

The lights come on, siren wails.

He thinks, *Do I run?*

He pulls over. The police car races past him, blows through a red light, cuts across an intersection, and pulls into a Krispy Kreme.

He pulls back onto the road. Deep breaths. He reaches the Budget Inn. No spots available near the street. He parks in a spot in the middle of the parking lot. He takes the luggage out of the trunk, finds room 203, knocks.

The door opens. A white man, beard, dirty clothes, answers the door, waves him in. He steps through the door into a short hallway. The man who answered the door closes it and is standing behind him. He walks forward, expecting to see two queen beds and the set-up of a typical hotel room. Around the corner two uniformed police officers point guns at two Hispanic men on their knees.

Panic.

He turns to run.

The white man with the beard pulls a gun from beneath his shirt.

He puts his hands up. Heart racing.

My little Carolina is all he thinks.

Miranda Rights.

Back of a police car.

Jail.

Stripped.

Searched.

Bars.

He sits for a long time. At least fifteen other men are in his cell. He stares at the ground that is littered with orange peels. One man cries. Another tells him to shut the fuck up.

Hours go by. He is moved to another cell. An angry black kid, no more than twenty years old paces back and forth. The kid says nothing, just paces. Occasionally the kid drops to the ground and does ten pushups.

He lies on his side on the concrete bed. He falls asleep thinking about his little Carolina.

It's morning. The black kid is gone. He's alone in this cell. He sits up. His shoulders are sore from sleeping on the concrete.

Two police officers come down the hall. They stop at his cell and mutter something. He can't hear what they said. He is waiting for his phone call. He is waiting to see the judge. The officers leave.

All day this happens. People walk to his cell, stop, mutter, and walk away.

An officer brings him a tray of food.

He thinks about his little girl. He thinks about what he will say to the judge. He wonders what happened to the other two men who got arrested with him. He wonders what they will say to the judge.

Another night comes and goes.

A white female officer and a Hispanic male officer come to his cell. They handcuff and shackle him. They bring him to an interrogation room with a large two-way mirror.

They leave him alone in the room.

Ten minutes go by. The female officer returns. She has a clipboard with a yellow pad of paper. She speaks, "What is your name?"

He doesn't know the answer. For the last two years people have been calling him Frank. He says, "Frank."

"What is your last name?" the officer sternly asks.

Again, he doesn't know the answer. He says nothing. He looks at her with pleading eyes.

"Do you know your last name?" she asks again.

He starts to panic. He stands. He speaks. He is angry. "I want a lawyer. I have the right to a lawyer."

The officer lessens her harsh tone, "Please sit down."

The door opens. Two more officers enter. They take him by the shoulders, forcing him to sit.

From inside the two-way mirror someone wails.

He looks back at the mirror. The sound vanishes. He sits.

He is never given an opportunity to speak with a lawyer. He is never given an opportunity to see a judge.

A police officer makes an introduction. "My name is Arty. We're going for a ride."

He is put in the back of a police van. Arty and another male officer are in the front of the van. Neither man is wearing a uniform, but he trusts that they are, in fact, police officers.

They drive all day and through the night. He falls asleep in the back of the van. He is still shackled. He doesn't know where they are going.

They eventually arrive. He's still not sure where they are but knows by the landscape that they must be somewhere in the Northeast. The officers open the doors of the van and lead him into a mental hospital. White walls, white ceramic floors. The smell of people who would rather die than live. Handsome men and pretty women in white coats and nursing uniforms hurry down halls and in and out of rooms.

He is led to a room. Shackles are taken off. Arty looks him in the eye, nods, and leaves.

The room has padded walls. There is a bed, much more comfortable than the concrete one he's been sleeping on. He sits.

He doesn't know what state he is in. He is hungry. He doesn't know why he has been brought here.

A nurse comes in and checks his vital signs. She leads him down the hall to an exam room and weighs him. A male nurse enters. The female nurse leaves.

"Remove your clothing," the male nurse instructs.

He takes off his clothing and lies down on the table.

A male doctor enters the room.

The doctor and the nurse examine his body. They make notes on a clipboard. They pause to examine a scar on his knee. They examine the tattoos on his arms. They say "Mmm," and write for a long time. The doctor leaves. The nurse says, "You can get dressed now," and leaves.

Another female nurse enters the room.

"Follow me," she says. They walk across the hospital to another room.

She leads him to sit in a chair. A different doctor comes in.

"Open your mouth," the doctor says.

He complies. The doctor examines his teeth. He puts pieces of plastic in his mouth and tells him to bite down. The nurse puts a heavy chest guard on him. They leave the room. X-rays are taken.

When they are finished, he is led back to the padded room, where a hot tray of terribly delicious hospital food waits for him. He inhales it.

Hours go by. He lies on the bed, clutching himself, wishing his little Carolina was in his arms. He drifts in and out of sleep.

Another doctor enters the room.

"Follow me please."

They walk to another wing of the hospital. He thinks to himself that it's weird he hasn't been shackled since he's been here.

The doctor sits him in a comfortable, office-like room. Unlike the rest of the stark hospital, this room has oak walls, leather chairs, and bookshelves.

The doctor asks, "Do you know why you've been brought here?"

"No."

"You are suffering from amnesia," the doctor explains.

"No."

"Your name is Charles Adam DiBella. You are from Morton, New Jersey. You have a wife and three children. Do you remember?" The doctor goes on.

"What? No! My name is Frank. I'm from Miami, Florida. I have a wife and a daughter named Carolina."

"Mr. DiBella, you've been missing for nearly a year and a half. It was assumed you were dead. We have your death certificate, cremation records, pictures of you with your family, medical records." The doctor motions to indicate the contents of files stacked upon his desk.

Panic sets in. No. He wants to go home.

The doctor lays down a stack of pictures.

He leans forward. He picks up the first one. It is of two white children and a white German Shepherd. He shakes his head. He picks up a second picture. His heart sinks. There he is, in the photograph. His arm is around a familiar woman with a gentle smile. He thinks, *My wife?* There are his beautiful children. He still can't remember their names, but he knows their faces.

He speaks.

"Where are they?"

The doctor speaks.

"They are here. Do you want them to come in?"

"Yes."

The doctor hits a button on his desk. A buzz. "You can let them in now."

The door opens behind him. He stands.

"Daddy! *Daddy!*" Tears, joy, a miracle.

My mother and dad grip each other tightly. They cry in each other's arms. My brother and I cling to his legs. My sister grips him from the back. The happiness, the relief, the joy. Even though I am twelve years old, he picks me up. He hugs me. I breathe in his aftershave, his cigarette smoke, I cling to his neck. I love him and this is a miracle.

He comes home with us. Our dog barks and jumps.

A few days later he remembers our names. He remembers our home.

His new wife and his baby daughter come. I love Carolina with all my heart. I hold her and play with her. She is my baby sister. Her mother is like a long-lost aunt. She is kind and loves our family.

Tears, happiness, joy.

"Kristy," my brother was standing over me. "We have to be at the bus stop in five minutes."

I stumbled out of bed. I was giddy and my mind was cloudy, but I was late for school. Sleepy-eyed, I pulled a hoodie over my baggy t-shirt, and slipped my feet into cheap plastic flip-flops. I staggered out the front door, holding my pajama pants up so they wouldn't drag on the ground and get wet. I just made it onto the bus. I sat in the brown leather seat and examined the skin lines of the leather. My head felt heavy. I was moving, and was awake enough to have made it to the bus stop, but my brain was still asleep.

I arrived at school. I expelled a great deal of energy to hoist myself up the stairs and through the front doors.

I was standing in the hallway. Cliques were yapping their morning chatter. A wet shoe screeched as it turned a corner, and a locker door slammed shut.

I collapsed to the ground and began screaming, "He's dead, he's dead, *he's dead!*"

I cried hysterically.

My peers came to a halt and stared. Someone ran to get a teacher. I was sobbing uncontrollably as a hundred people whispered.

"He's dead, he's dead!" I sobbed loudly.

A teacher crouched by my side. Another teacher was ushering students into classrooms. People looked over their shoulders as they were herded away from me.

The bell rang. The hall emptied. The guidance counselor was sitting on the floor next to me.

I cried uncontrollably for a long time. Eventually I made it to her office. I continued crying. I told her my dream. I told her how real it was. I told her how much I needed it to be real. At that point, all I wanted was to be with my dad. Suicide seemed like a good option.

I told the guidance counselor, "I just want to go be with my dad."

She perceived that as a serious suicide threat. We talked for a very long time, until she decided she didn't have to call for further intervention.

Eventually my slightly intoxicated mother came to pick me up. I rolled my eyes while she pretended to listen intently to the guidance counselor, who explained her concerns about my mental health. My mother took me home. I walked through the empty house. It was nothing like the end of my dream. No one was happy. It was a mess. My mother's boyfriend, Evan, was sitting on the couch, in the spot where my dad had died. It was ten a.m. and he was watching porn on the big-screen TV. A line of coke was on the coffee table and he was cracked out of his mind.

I went in my room, closed the door and lay face down. I spent the rest of the day sobbing from my soul, begging my dad to come home. Eventually I cried myself to sleep.

Hours later I woke up in the darkness with a debilitating migraine. I was paralyzed. My brain was mostly awake, but my arms and legs couldn't move. I felt a hand on my chest. For a moment I thought someone might be trying to shake me awake. I realized it was Evan. But then I realized his hand was inching down my abdomen. I focused every ounce of energy in me to scream or call out for help, but nothing came out of my mouth. Evan's hand approached my pubic bone. All at once, my brain connected with my mouth and I let out a howl. He instantly withdrew his hand, stumbled backward, and shuffled out of my room.

My heart was beating out of my chest. I sat up in bed, trying to make sense of what had just happened. I stood, and walked over to my door. I closed it, then checked the lock over and over. I jiggled the door handle and pulled on the door at least twenty times. I went back to my bed and started crying again.

Daddy, come save me. Daddy, I need your help. Daddy, why did you leave me?

I felt dirty and scared, and my throat was raw, and my nose was running from crying so much. But that night I didn't know what else to do.

The next day I arrived at school. While walking down the hall, I could hear people whispering, "That girl is psycho."

"I heard she tried to kill herself last night."

"I hope they put her in a mental institution."

39

Incredible Luck

I came home from school and there was a gold car in the driveway. I'd never seen it before, but had a feeling I was in trouble. I walked up the wooden steps and into the house. Evan's wife, Shelby, was sitting at the kitchen table with a young, thin woman with curly brown hair and a beige top. My mother was opening cabinets in the kitchen, pointing to various types of food.

"Hi Kristy, how are you?" the stranger said to me.

I was startled that she knew my name.

She asked my mother, "Would it be okay to speak to Kristy alone?"

My mother said, "Of course! I have nothing to hide!"

The woman took me in my brother's bedroom. She said she was with the Department of Social Services. They had received a call and were concerned about my wellbeing. She asked me to tell her about what it was like living in my house.

"Well, I, um…" I stuttered. I was extremely nervous. *Who was this beautiful, well-put-together, professional-looking stranger? How can I straightforwardly tell her what was happening?* I felt embarrassed and couldn't organize my thoughts.

She asked me if I had enough to eat, and I said sometimes I did not. She asked me if my mother used drugs, and I said I didn't know. I knew she was disabled, and I knew she had prescriptions. At the time, I genuinely did not know if she was abusing the pills, or if her behavior was a normal reaction to the pills. I had no idea if she was doing illegal drugs. Lastly, this lovely person asked me if I was being sexually abused. I froze.

"No," I lied.

My mother received $1,450 a month each for me and my brother from Social Security survivors benefits. Because of the investigation, my mother had to prove she was spending some of that on my brother and me. Allegations had been made that she was not using the money to purchase things like clothing and food for us.

My mother made it a point to purchase raffle tickets that were being sold at a local church. There would be a drawing to win spots at summer camps. My mother was very specific about making sure we got receipts for the raffle tickets. They were five dollars each, and hundreds of parents participated in the drawing.

My mother, Evan, my brother, and I went together to the church the night of the drawing. As I took my place in the pew, I imagined Evan's wedding with Shelby, and wondered if it took place in a church like this one. I hoped God or the church would make Evan burst into flames for the night he had his hands on me. I still wasn't sure what had happened, but I felt like it must have been a sin.

"You can choose two summer camps," my mother instructed me and my brother.

My brother chose football and baseball. I chose horseback riding and drama.

The raffle announcers said they would do boys' sports first. Tiny pieces of white paper, folded into squares, were placed inside a large clear plastic barrel, which was attached to a crank. Baseball was first. The barrel was spun, and the woman leading the raffle reached her hand in. She pulled out a number, read it, and a family in the crowded room erupted into a cheer. Everyone else in the room politely clapped.

The woman repeated the process, reading off winning numbers for soccer, lacrosse, hockey, wrestling, golf, track, and swimming. Finally, the last boy's event was announced. It was the most anticipated event, football. The barrel spun, and the number was called. It wasn't my brother's and I was disappointed for him.

Some of the families in the crowd gathered their things and began emptying out of the church, despite an announcement from the podium asking everyone to stay for the duration of the assembly. After a third of the crowd left anyway, another announcement was made that we were going to move on to the summer camps for girls.

She read off the winners of the swimming, field hockey, volleyball, cheerleading, dance, soccer, and track camps. At that point boredom overtook me and I stopped paying attention. The barrel spun, and they called a number.

"Kristy," my mother snapped at me. "You won!"

I thought I hadn't heard her correctly.

"You won the summer camp for drama!" she confirmed.

A couple slow, unenthusiastic claps followed, but I could tell everyone in the room was growing impatient.

The barrel spun again, and the hundreds of pieces of paper tumbled around. It was the last and most anticipated summer camp for girls: horseback-riding. The woman reached in again for the very last slot, and again called another number.

"What?" my mother said excitedly.

There was muttering throughout the room. My mother brought up the second ticket. The facilitator looked down at the piece of paper, then looked up and confirmed that, despite astronomically small odds, I had won both drawings.

At the end of the drawing, my mother approached the lectern to speak to the women running the event.

"I have two children," my mother said. "Would it be possible to trade in one of the raffles my daughter won for a week of camp for my son?"

I didn't understand what she was doing. I felt so lucky to have won both drawings, and she was insistently trying to give one of my winning tickets to my brother. I felt bad that my brother didn't win, but also felt that I had won fairly.

Another parent cut in, "It's really unfair that she won two weeks, when hundreds of children entered the drawing."

I felt attacked and ashamed that I had won. But then the woman running the event said, "There is no rule against a child winning two slots." Then turning to my mother, she said, "And the winning slots are nontransferable. If you want to forfeit your daughter's winning slot, that is up to you, but I cannot exchange it for a slot for your son."

I felt a huge relief and felt like someone had stuck up for me.

Several nights later I was in my bedroom listening to music, trying on a jean skirt Carissa let me borrow, and painting my eyelids and lips black with makeup Lily loaned me. Evan was at our house to have dinner and then get drunk and high with my mother. I hated it, but that's what became normal.

"Kristy," my mother called from down the hallway, "Come eat!"

My mother was acting particularly flirtatious, fawning over Evan, and it was nauseating to watch. I was sitting at the table when my mother leaned in close to my face and asked, "Have you fucked any of the little boys at your school yet?"

"*Mom!*" I shouted. I could feel my face turning red with rage. I stood up from the table, violently pushing her away from me.

Evan laughed, "Haha, yeah, you're really turning into a little slut." He reached out and pulled up the short skirt I was wearing.

"Mom, get him the fuck out of the house!" I demanded, pulling away from him.

She raged back at me, "This is my house! Don't you dare ever think you can tell me who I can have in my house! I'm the mom!"

I stormed down the hallway and into my bedroom. I gathered up my blanket, pillow, and a couple articles of clothing. I threw everything over my shoulder and stomped back through the dining area, where Evan and my mother were laughing about making me so angry.

I descended the spiral stairs, made my way through the basement, and went into the storm room. I started lifting boxes out of the way and cleared enough space to lay down an old futon mattress that had been sitting in the basement for years. *This will be my new room,* I thought, *as far away from her as I can get.* I spent the rest of the night organizing the room in the basement. It had a bare concrete floor, no windows, a door that opened to the garage, a door that opened to the rest of the basement, and a heavy storm door that opened to the driveway. The walls had no insulation, and the ceiling had wires and pipes running in different directions. The air was damp. But being away from my mother, who was ascending into madness before my eyes, was my only priority.

In the weeks leading up to summer camp, I couldn't contain my anticipation. I felt like getting away from my mother would solve a lot of my problems. I compulsively began to pack, unpack, repack, and organize my bags over and over. I spent hours imagining what it might be like at camp. I didn't know what to expect, assuming it'd be like scenes from cartoons on Nickelodeon. I fantasized that I was going to live in a cabin in the woods forever, and I would never have to come back to my mother's house again.

My mother drove me to the summer camp. It was approximately a three hour drive, and the anticipation made it feel like a year in the car.

I was in my cabin and other girls were unpacking their backpacks. A girl with medium-length, deep-brown hair and stunning green eyes was hanging a Blink-182 poster above her bed. We immediately hit it off and became inseparable. Her name was Alyse, and she told me she had attended that summer camp every summer, for the entire summer, since second grade. All of the camp counselors knew her, and she had a very good reputation as a responsible, hard-working, rule-abiding camper.

When I first got there, I wanted to seem cool. Almost immediately I had a lot of problems with one specific girl in my cabin named Kaylee. I quickly found out her mom was in charge of the entire summer camp. She was a spoiled, immature, selfish girl. We'd occasionally bicker, but mostly I stayed away from her.

My first week was my horseback-riding week, and I was elated to get started. The first day we were introduced to the camp. I spent all of my free time with Alyse. I loved that she was creative, easy to talk to, and accepted me for who I was. We began staying up late every night and pushed our beds together so we could talk and play games. The camp counselors saw me as a bad influence on Alyse and suggested to her that she move to another cabin. She declined, which made me feel like she really valued our friendship. Over the next two weeks, we ate every meal together, swam in the lake, and sang around a campfire. She told me all about her family, and I told her a little bit about mine. We were on different activity schedules, so during our activities we weren't together. I didn't want to seem desperate, and I didn't want Alyse to know I was kind of a loser at home. I only had three friends, and I was definitely at the bottom of the pecking order with them, because they'd all been friends their whole lives, and only adopted me into their friend group in seventh grade.

While I was at the barn, Alyse was on her mountain-biking week. I was committed to learning everything I could about the horses. Each time the owner of the barn asked for something to be done, I was the first to shoot my hand in the air and volunteer. If we were supposed to complete a task, I consistently finished the task the best and the fastest.

Finally, it was time for us to actually ride the horses. I was taught how to post, which I picked up extremely quickly. We were told to complete an obstacle course, which involved riding our horses through barrels and over wooden planks, then dismounting and leading the horses through a series of tasks. I completed the entire course in less than half the time as any other girl.

One morning when my group of campers arrived at the barn, the owner pulled me aside and introduced me to two girls who were about my age.

"Follow me," the girl with blonde hair and freckles waved.

Together the three of us climbed a ladder into the hay loft of the barn. Through the cracks in the boards we could see the other campers and the owner, who was teaching them about mucking.

"Won't we get in trouble?" I whispered. I didn't want to miss any important lessons.

"No," the taller brunette girl said. "Miss Shelly told us to bring you up here."

After a couple of minutes Miss Shelly led the campers out to the riding ring.

"Okay, let's go!" the blonde girl said excitedly.

We descended the ladder. The two girls taught me how to put a saddle on a horse, and then how to put on a bridle. I practiced two more times, on two more horses.

"Ready?" the brunette girl asked.

They instructed me to mount the middle horse, then the two of them mounted horses in front of and behind me. We spent the entire day, about seven hours, on top of our horses. We rode through rivers, up mountains, and through huge open fields. We stopped only a couple of times to eat, or to see an old, abandoned structure in the woods.

It was such a wonderful day that I truly forgot who I was. I forgot that my mother's boyfriend sometimes molested me. I forgot that my mother sometimes didn't feed me, or that she hit me, or even that my dad died. I felt like I was on the best adventure of my entire life. I felt free, safe, and warm from the inside out. I felt like the horse was an extension of my body. I felt like those two girls were my long-lost sisters.

That went on for the remainder of the week. Each day I'd arrive at the barn, hide in the hay loft, then spend the whole day with the two girls and our horses, exploring the woods. At night I was thrilled to tell Alyse every detail, and to hear all about her day as well.

The following week, on Sunday, we were supposed to get introduced to our next activity. I woke up, not realizing my time at the barn had come to an end. I followed Alyse to the chow hall. When we were almost there, I realized Miss Shelly was standing in the doorway of the cabin the camp leader slept in. I raced up to her to say hi.

Before I reached her, she turned around and saw me.

"Kristy!" she exclaimed. "Good morning. I have something I want to ask you."

"Good morning, Miss Shelly," I heaved, slightly out of breath. "What is it?"

"You've been doing so well at the barn, and I've been so happy to have you each day. I was wondering if you wanted to switch activities this week. Instead of going to drama, do you want to spend another week at the barn?"

"*Yes!*" I shouted so loud, I must have woke up anyone in the camp who was still asleep.

"Great! Enjoy your day today, and I'll see you tomorrow!" she cheerfully told me as she waved and walked toward her pickup truck.

I turned and bolted up the hill to catch up with Alyse and tell her the good news.

The following week I learned more and more from Miss Shelly and the two girls. I learned that both girls had been adopted. They lived with Miss Shelly, competed regularly in horse competitions, each had their own horse in the barn, and went to private school. In my entire life I'd never felt more accepted and wanted.

On my last day Miss Shelly left the campers with a barn hand. She mounted a horse, and we all rode together to the river. With very little prying, I openly told Miss Shelly about my life at home. I told her how much I missed my dad, and about my mother's married boyfriend. I told her about failing in school, and how I had no friends. I opened up to her, and she put her arms out and gave me a hug that made me feel like she had gathered up my broken pieces and was putting me back together. I told her everything, except about being molested. I wanted to tell her, but because the two girls were there, I didn't want to say something inappropriate that would make them not want to be my friends anymore.

Before leaving on the bus back to camp, Miss Shelly asked me to write down my phone number, so that she could stay in touch with me. Leaving her, and leaving the horses made me feel empty. But emptiness was the norm back in my normal life at home.

On the final day of the summer camp, everyone's parents were coming. We were having a picnic lunch where the parents were supposed to sit with their children under the massive covering of the chow hall, and we were to show off our art projects and the progress we had made in our sport or activity.

When I woke up, I went to the chow hall for breakfast, returned to my cabin, and finished packing my clothes and other personal items. Parents began arriving mid-morning, and then activities started. Alyse's dad arrived, and he was completely different from what I had expected. He was thinner, shorter, and younger than I thought he would be.

I climbed upon a rock and watched as other girls led their parents around, showing them the campfire, the flagpole, the lake, the cabins, and other spots. An hour later it was lunch time, and I followed everyone into the chow hall.

Alyse introduced her father, "This is my dad!"

"Hi," he extended his hand. "What's your name?"

"Kristy," I responded, and shook his hand.

"Where are your parents?" Alyse asked innocently.

I didn't talk in extreme detail with Alyse about my mother. At the time, I didn't know why my mother was so spaced out all the time. I had told her that my dad died, but I think at that moment, with excitement in the air, she just forgot. "I don't know. We live really far away. Maybe my mother got lost." I hoped that that is what had happened but knew it probably wasn't. I ate lunch, and then hugged Alyse goodbye, not sure if I would ever see her again. I watched her dad load her bags into the back of his pickup truck, and then I waved goodbye with one hand while thumbing her address and phone number, written on a special piece of stationery her parents sent her, in my pocket.

At the beginning of my stay at the summer camp, I had had a problem with a girl named Kaylee. Her mom was the director of the camp. As the afternoon dragged on, and more and more children drove away with their parents, Kaylee's mom approached me. "Is it possible your mom forgot what day to pick you up?"

I didn't know.

"How about we go in the office and you give her a call?" Kaylee's mom suggested.

I followed Kaylee's mom into the office and gave her my home phone number. She dialed, and then handed me the phone.

It rang and rang. I stood there and prayed that she would pick up, but she didn't. Kaylee's mom took the phone from me and hung it up. "Do you have anyone else you can call to come pick you up?"

I could only think of one person: Evan's wife. I dialed her phone number. On the third ring, she picked up.

"Hello?" I was relieved to hear anyone's voice on the other end of the line.

"Shelby?" I said into the receiver.

"Kristy?" She sounded confused.

"My mother was supposed to come pick me up from summer camp today. She was supposed to be here a couple of hours ago. I need someone to come pick me up," I pleaded with her.

"Where are you?" She asked.

I handed the phone to Kaylee's mom, and watched as Kaylee's mom explained where the camp was. After a couple minutes she hung up the phone.

"Who was that?" Kaylee's mom asked me.

"That was my mother's boyfriend's wife." I blurted, not realizing how wild it sounded.

"Um, okay," she said uneasily. "She said she doesn't have enough money for gas to get up here. She said she'll call back in a couple of minutes."

I felt embarrassed. I thought I hid the truth that I was poor pretty well for the past two weeks. But there was no hiding this. Not coming to get your kid from summer camp is pretty bad. Your mom's boyfriend having a wife is pretty bad. Being stranded in the woods in upstate New York, and not knowing anyone with enough money for gas to come get you, all of those things were pretty bad.

I waited outside, alone, for several more hours. It was the end of summer, so when the sun was setting, it was chilly and mosquitoes were biting my legs. I didn't care. I watched the camp counselors stack up chairs in the chow hall and move boxes of unsold chips and candy out of the commissary cabin.

Finally, Shelby's beat-up, rusty car clanked over the dirt road that led to the entrance of the camp. I was both relieved and mortified to see her. Kaylee's mom met Shelby outside. I gathered up my backpack and loose articles and hung my head as I walked across the grass toward her.

"You ready?" Shelby looked at me disgracefully.

"Yeah," I squeaked quietly.

She helped me with my bigger bag, and I got in the front seat of her car. She got in and the driver's side door slammed shut. She lit a cigarette. I'd never seen her smoke before.

"I found these cigarettes in my house," she said. "I have no idea who they belong to."

The drive back was long, and through narrow mountain roads Shelby never asked why my mother hadn't come to get me. She also never said anything about where her husband was.

When we arrived at my mother's house, Evan's car was parked in the driveway. Shelby pulled in.

"Thanks." I said, as I slipped out the passenger's side door. Shelby popped the trunk open, and I pulled my heavy bag out and onto the rocks of the driveway. I dragged the bag off to the side and retrieved my backpack and a lighter bag from the back seat. Before closing the door, I said, "Sorry." Shelby just looked at me, and I perceived the message to be, *We both know what's going on here.* I moved back, away from the car, and Shelby rolled backward, then chirped the wheels as she sped up the hill, rolled through a stop sign, and made a right turn out of the neighborhood.

I put the backpack on my back, threw the lighter bag over my shoulder, and lugged the heavy bag over the driveway. I pushed the unlocked heavy storm door open, and dragged my things inside. I left them in a pile in the corner. I took a look around. Everything was the same as I had left it. There was one week left of summer vacation, and then I would be starting high school.

I lay face down on the futon mattress on the floor of the basement and breathed in the musty, moldy, moist air trapped in the fibers. I closed my eyes. The ceiling fan started rocking back and forth, and I could hear the sound of sex coming from my mother's bedroom, which was directly above mine. I gathered pillows around my head, trying to block out the noise, but it was too loud to ignore.

The next day I woke up and came upstairs. Shelby and my mother were sitting at the kitchen table drinking coffee. My mother paused when she saw me coming through the living room. I walked past the two of them and used the bathroom. When I came back out, Shelby and my mother were laughing at Jerry Springer. The episode was about affairs and secret pregnancies.

Unexpectedly, the phone began ringing.

"Hello?" my mother picked up, then turned and stared at me. She continued, "Yes, this is her. Miss who? Miss Shelly? Mhmm. Mhmm. Yes, I understand. No. No, thank you. No, we're not interested. No." My mother abruptly hung up the phone.

"Miss Shelly?" I was so excited that she had called. "What did she say?"

"She wanted to know if I would consider letting you live with her and go to boarding school up there." My mother seemed annoyed.

"Really? That would be incredible! Please, Mom, please! She was such a nice lady. She has two daughters who she adopted who are the same age as me, and—"

"Are you out of your fucking mind? If I let you go, I would lose your Social Security check, and then I wouldn't be able to pay the mortgage!" She was becoming irate.

"But—"

But she immediately unpaused the TV and turned the volume all the way up.

I returned to my room in the basement, shut the door, and lay on the futon mattress. I pulled the blankets up to my chin and bit down. Then I started violently shaking my head from side to side. The feeling made me instantly feel tired. I just wanted to go back to sleep. I was knocking my brain around in my skull. I did it for about three minutes before I fell asleep.

40

Cheerleading

The next day I woke up with a migraine. There was only one week left of summer vacation, and then I'd be starting high school. I lay in bed and strained my hearing. Evan's voice boomed from the kitchen.

I decided to get out of bed, get dressed, and walk to my new high school, which was approximately three miles away. I was excited for high school to start because several school districts had come together, and I thought it would be a great opportunity to make new friends. I was curious to see the building. I expected to get there, look around, then walk back to my house. When I arrived, I was surprised to see a lot of people were there. I walked around the back of the school to the football stadium. There were about a hundred boys doing pushups, laps, and stretches.

"Hey!" an adult voice shouted at me.

I turned to look.

"Are you looking for the cheerleading tryouts?" The adult asked me. "They're in the cafeteria. Go through those double doors and straight down the hallway. You can't miss it."

"Okay, thank you," I said as I made my way toward the double doors he had pointed at. I'd never considered becoming a cheerleader. But I had nothing else to do, so I decided to have a look at what was going on.

In the cafeteria about sixty girls were stretching, and an older, athletic woman with short blonde hair was walking around with a clipboard and a megaphone. The megaphone seemed like overkill.

She saw me and snapped, "Line up against the wall."

I complied.

Over the next week, I came every day. We learned complicated routines. Some of the girls could do backflips and front flips. Very few could do a full split. Because of martial arts I was able to do the full split. I learned that the woman leading the tryouts was the school nurse.

When I came home at night, I watched *Bring It On* on repeat, and did my best to mimic everything they did. At practice the following day, I would demonstrate techniques I had seen in the movie with spectacular precision.

I put every ounce of effort I had into learning everything and keeping up with the girls who'd clearly been cheerleading their entire childhoods. Because of my positive experience that summer with Miss Shelly, I was eager to find a positive female role model and a group of girls I would be able to trust and call my friends.

On the final day, we were supposed to perform a routine we had practiced all week. We'd been broken into smaller groups. I quickly realized the group I was in was the reject group. The girls were awkward, or annoying, or ugly, or didn't work hard throughout the week. I watched all of the other groups' routines. They had high ponytails with bright bows, and matching outfits, and crisp white sneakers. And for the first time that week, they were all using shiny pompoms.

I looked down at my dirty Walmart-brand sneakers, my sweatpants with a hole in the crotch, and my striped T-shirt that was covered in stains. For the first time that week, I realized I wasn't dressed for the part of a cheerleader. I would have, if I'd known I was supposed to, and if I had had access to cute clothes or bows. In that moment, I wished, harder than I'd ever wished for food, to have pompoms. I realized that no matter how straight my split was, and no matter how many moves I learned, without the pompoms and the bows and the matching outfits, I was never going to be chosen.

When my group, the reject group, was called, I swallowed hard. But I went out and did my best. When the music started, I did each move. When I spun around, though, I realized that none of the other girls were in sync. Some of them had even given up completely and weaseled off to the side. I decided I was going to finish strong regardless. I flexed and jumped and shot my arms out and, on the last beat of the song, landed in a perfect split.

"Thank you, ladies," the woman with short hair said. "Get a drink and come back here in ten minutes. We'll announce who made the varsity squad, who made junior varsity, and if your name doesn't get called, you'll be welcome to try out for the winter squad in three months."

When we all came back, the prettiest girls with the highest ponytails were squeezing each other's hands, bouncing up and down in the front row. The names were called. Every girl from every other small group was placed on either varsity or junior varsity. Every single girl from my group, the reject group, wasn't called.

I walked home alone.

Our first day of high school was a Friday. I was sitting in my first-period class, which was math class. The morning program came on, which was a news-like program made by seniors in the school. They read off all the names of the people who had made it onto varsity or junior varsity in various sports. When they came to the cheerleaders, I sank low in my chair, remembering how disappointed I had been the day before.

Suddenly, the announcer on TV said my name!

"Congratulations, Kristy," someone sitting behind me patted me on the shoulder.

"Cool! Congratulations!" more people said, sounding sincere.

I perked up in my chair. *Maybe the nurse changed her mind? Maybe she knew how much I needed to belong? Wow! What a nice lady!* I thought to myself.

"Excuse me," I raised my hand. "May I please go to the nurse's office?"

"Of course," my teacher said to me in an oddly compliant manner.

I stood up and left the classroom. In the hallway I passed two other people I didn't know, who congratulated me. I was startled. This instant popularity was weird, but definitely nice. I was smiling ear to ear. In my head I was going over how to thank the nurse for giving me this opportunity. I burst through the door, prepared to give her a hug!

"Hi!" I exclaimed. "I just heard the morning announcement. Tha—"

She cut me off. "I made a mistake in the Excel spreadsheet and pulled the column too far over. You're not on the squad."

The expression 'hit by a ton of bricks' is sometimes overused, but honest to God, in that moment, that's exactly how I felt.

For the remainder of the day, people kept congratulating me, and I kept having to tell them it was a mistake, I hadn't made the squad. After a while, it seemed like they were angry at me, like I had purposely deceived them, only to make them look stupid when I told them it wasn't true.

Oh well, I thought, *being popular and well-liked and having friends is probably overrated.*

I went home that day and watched *Bring It On* one more time, so I could let myself cry alone.

The next day was Saturday and I slept in late, only to be woken up by someone pounding on the storm door. I was groggy but got out of bed and opened the door.

"Kristy," I couldn't see who it was because I didn't have my contacts in, but I could tell from the voice that it was Lily's boyfriend, TJ.

"Hey, what's up?" I was confused about why he was here.

"My grandma dropped me off, but I can't get a hold of Lily. I think she might be grounded or something. Can I use your computer for a few minutes?" He asked.

"Yeah, but hurry up. My psycho mom enacted this new rule where none of my friends are allowed on her property," I explained to him.

"Okay, it'll just be five minutes," he said as he came in and powered up the computer.

I sat back down on my bed and noticed I had a pounding headache. I lay back down and pulled my blanket over my head.

When TJ was done, he stood up from the computer. He still couldn't contact Lily and was going to hang out with other friends. I said bye and told him to pull the storm door shut when he left. When he was gone, I went back to sleep.

A few hours later there was another knock on my door.

I got out of bed again and answered.

"My grandma's going to pick me up from the rock soon. Do you want to walk with me?" TJ asked.

I thought, *I've been asleep all day. I should get some fresh air*. "Sure," I said. I motioned to be quiet, strained my hearing, and realized Evan and my mother were upstairs. "My contact lenses are upstairs. I don't want to go get them because I don't want to have to deal with my mother and her boyfriend."

"We'll only be gone for a couple minutes," TJ whined. "You won't need them."

TJ and I set out toward the rock. I was barefoot, blind, and wearing PJ pants and a T-shirt. We walked and talked about his high school. He lived a few towns over and wasn't starting until next week. I told him he was lucky he had extra time off. Mid-conversation TJ suddenly jumped behind a bush. I froze. I heard pattering noises on the concrete.

"You stupid whore!" I heard Lily shouting.

"TJ?" I blindly looked around. I had no idea what was going on.

Lily's voice was closer. "You fucked TJ!" she shouted.

"What? No I didn't!" I defended myself.

"TJ, get the fuck out here!" Lily demanded.

TJ came out from behind the bush and Lily started smacking him.

"Babe, stop!" TJ pleaded.

"You cheated on me!" she went on.

"No, I didn't!" TJ said.

"Look at your neck. There are hickeys all over it!" she continued to shout. Then she turned her attention to me. "I'm going to kick your ass!"

I stepped back. My vision was terrible, and I couldn't see her swing her fist, which collided with my head. It felt like a gentle tap, and for a split second I had to figure out if she was joking, or if she just didn't know how to fight. I realized she didn't know how to fight but was going to attempt to strike me again. I raised my leg and roundhouse-kicked her in the head.

"Kristy!" TJ shouted. He jumped in the way and pushed Lily away from me. I could hear them fighting and moving farther away from me.

I walked back to my house, went upstairs past my mother and her boyfriend, and put my contacts in. I checked the side of my face where Lily had tapped me. There wasn't a mark or anything.

That night on AOL, I received threatening messages from Lily's older sister, which said she was going to kick my ass. The next day I received threatening messages from Carissa and Lindsay. I prayed that their anger would dissipate before school started again.

When I walked into school on Monday, I felt like everyone was staring at me. Near the front doors, in front of the main office, I saw Lily.

"Look at that slut!" Lily shouted and pointed at me.

My face got hot. Everyone stopped what they were doing and looked to where Lily was pointing.

"I'm going to kick your ass again, just like I did over the weekend!" Lily exclaimed.

I was momentarily confused. Did she have the same memory as I did about what had happened? She tapped me, I kicked her, TJ stepped in the way, and that was it. No ass kicking had occurred.

Lily began stomping toward me.

"Fuck you, Lily. If I fight you, I'd get herpes!" I shouted back.

"Kristen!" The vice principal shouted. "Get in my office right this second! Lily, get in Mr. Serro's office!"

The vice principal told me to shut the door and sit behind her desk, and she began scolding me.

"I didn't start the fight," I said.

"I don't care who started it. You can't say that Lily has herpes. That's defamation of character. It's illegal. I should call the police."

"It's not defamation of character! The herpes is all over her face. It's not defamation if it's a fact!" I fought back.

"Detention every day for two weeks," the vice principal said.

After that, each day at school became more and more of a battle. Lily's sister spread rumors about me that I had had an abortion over the summer and slept with all these different boys who I'd never even met. All her friends believed her, and the rumors became facts that everyone was absolutely sure of. Carissa and Lindsay completely sided with Lily, and I became the outcast.

I had no idea where TJ went after he had left my house. If I'd had my contacts in, I would have been able to see the hickeys when he came back and asked me to go to the rock with him. Maybe then I would have been able to tell Lily, instead of being caught completely off-guard.

41

You Can't Sit with Us

Shortly after my fight with Lily, I was called into the guidance counselor's office. She wanted to talk to me. She asked me how I was feeling regarding the loss of my father, and she told me there was a group that met every other week. It was only for students who had lost a parent, and I was invited to it.

I gave it a shot. At a large conference table, I looked around and was surprised that there were a dozen other students in my school whose parents had passed away. Before this I had assumed I was the only person. I was relieved to have an opportunity to talk about my dad's death with people who had experienced something similar.

I spoke candidly about my dad's death. I was the only person whose parent had committed suicide—everyone else's parent had died either in an accident, from cancer, or a heart attack. I wanted to connect with those people though. Suicide was a different kind of loss, but at least they were people my age who were sad about the same thing.

    A couple days later I was called down to the guidance office again. Mrs. Golf sat me down and told me that "the group doesn't come together as well" when I was there, so I wasn't allowed to attend anymore. She said I could continue speaking with her individually if I felt it necessary. I was crushed. This had felt like an opportunity to connect with my peers and be heard. And after only one session, I had been kicked out. I didn't want to talk to an adult with a master's degree. I wanted to talk to kids my age who didn't know how they were going to pay for college. I wanted to talk to them about their remaining parent. I wanted to find out how their remaining parent was coping with the death, because I knew my mother wasn't coping well. I had so many questions and had gone into the group feeling really optimistic, excited, energized, and hopeful.

    I was so destitute when I was kicked out.

I felt completely alone.

42

My Only Friend

After the rumors about me, started by Lily's sister, spread at my school, people stayed pretty far away from me. One of the only people who would still talk to me was a girl named Candice. Within the first two weeks of school, the rumors became a plague I couldn't get away from. All of the bad kids in Lily and her sister's group of friends believed every word they said. Each day I heard more and more outrageous things about myself. Candice, who came from a different middle school, was assigned to be my science-lab partner on the first day of school. Her initial impression of me was that I was very nice. But as the rumors started circulating, I could tell she wanted to pull away from me.

"Do you know where Candice is?" my science teacher questioned me when she noticed she hadn't been in class that day.

"No idea," I responded.

"Okay, when you see her, could you please have her come to my office? I have a couple things I have to give her," she said.

The next day I saw her in the hallway. "Hi, Candice. Mrs. Jones has something for you and told me to tell you to go to her office as soon as you can."

"Okay, thanks!" she said.

"Why were you absent?" I asked.

"Well, I broke up with my boyfriend, and I was really sad about it. So my mom took a day off from work and we went to have lunch and got pedicures," she told me in a sweet and innocent tone.

I was baffled. I thought, *What? Your mom actually cares when bad things happen to you?* I could not comprehend that her mom did that. In my mind, and as far as I knew, I thought parents liked their children when they were babies and toddlers, but once they became preteens and teenagers, their parents hated them. It was incomprehensible to me that a parent would give advice and offer condolence when something bad happened, let alone actually take off from work. I didn't even know that people could take off from work for something like that. Worse, it had never occurred to me that an adult would offer guidance or could empathize. I stood there, speechless and bewildered, imagining the idea of an adult taking me out for lunch and intently listening to my thoughts and fears. I had no idea what a pedicure was. It sounded special.

Weeks later Candice was going to come over my house on Saturday to work on our science-fair project and have a sleepover. I was beyond elated. I raced home from school that Friday. I cleaned my bedroom from top to bottom and attempted to create a bedframe out of cinder blocks, so that my room would look a little more presentable. Near sunset, when I was done cleaning, I was in my backyard thinking of ways to catch bugs for our experiment when I saw something move.

It was a kitten! I was so excited!

My dad had built a wooden walkway, and the kitten ran underneath it. I started pulling up the planks. Finally, the little kitten, who was petrified, was cornered. I snagged it up and held it close to my chest.

It was orange with white stripes, a giant head, completely adorable, and I was in love.

I took it into my bedroom and decided to name it Odie.

The next day Candice came over. I couldn't wait to show her the kitten. When she arrived I said, "I have a surprise!"

She came in my bedroom and I moved some boxes where I knew the kitten was hiding.

"Awwwwww!" She gushed over the kitten. "I want one!"

"I could probably find more," I offered, trying to sound cool.

"Okay, I'll ask my mom," she said.

It was dinnertime, and of course Evan was there. I sat next to Evan, trying to put distance between him and Candice. My brother was across from us. My mother was at the stove. While she was cooking, Evan leaned in, "You girls having a sleepover?"

"Yeah!" Candice exclaimed.

"Are you going to sleep in bed with each other?" Evan pried. He reached his hand out, placing it uncomfortably on my shoulder.

The blood drained from my face and I was completely mortified. Candice swallowed and looked over at me.

Evan asked, "Are you girls going to experiment with each other?"

Candice slid her chair out. "Excuse me." Her voice was shaky and full of fear. She shuffled quickly through my house and down the stairs.

I followed her down, but she slammed my bedroom door shut.

Through the door I could hear her on her cellphone, "Mom, I need you to come get me."

I felt so bad at that moment. *Why me?* I thought. I slid down next to the door. I heard Candice hang up. "Candice?" I called. "Are you okay?"

"Yeah, I'm fine. I just need a minute," she said through the door.

I sat there feeling horrible, nauseous, and numb. I'd accepted that Evan did perverted, disgusting things to me in the night. I could handle that as long as it was just me. I'd accepted that that's all I was worth. But Candice was pure and white and clean. I felt so bad that he had scared her. My embarrassment pushed down on me, and I stayed crouched in the corner next to my door for about 15 minutes.

My dog started barking upstairs. I bolted up the stairs to the front door. Candice had gone out of my house through the storm door, and I watched as she got in her mom's sleek, black, luxury car in the driveway. It sat there for a moment, then rolled backward and pulled away.

"Kristy," my mother called behind me. "It's time to eat."

I looked back at the kitchen table. Evan was smirking and impenitent, and my mother was standing there, holding a pot from the stove.

I went out the front door, around the side of the house, and in through the storm door that led to my bedroom. I sat on my dusty old futon mattress, held my kitten, and cried. I prayed that Candice wasn't too hurt, and thought, *What is she going to tell the other kids at school?*

Later that day I went in my backyard, thinking that I had to make it up to her. I hunted and hunted, and after hours, right as the sun was about to disappear, I caught a frail black kitten. I was so proud. I thought, *Surely she'll still want to be my friend!*

I picked up the phone and dialed her number.

"Hello?" she said.

"Hi...Are you okay?" I asked.

"Yeah. I forgot my backpack," she said.

I looked over, and saw it sitting in the corner. I didn't even realize she had left it.

She asked, "Can I come pick it up tomorrow? I need it for school."

"Yeah, of course," I said.

She hung up.

In the afternoon the next day, I heard my dog barking upstairs. I opened the storm door to see Candice's mom's sleek car coming into the driveway. I picked up her backpack and the black kitten and made my way to the driveway.

"Oh, my goodness!" she squealed from the passenger's seat with the window rolled mostly down. I extended my hand with the backpack, but she snatched the kitten from me. "Mom! Can I keep it?"

Her mom smiled a gentle smile and nodded her head.

She gave the kitten to her mom, then returned to me and pulled her backpack through the window. "Thanks," she said. Before I could respond the window was rolling up, and I watched them roll out of the driveway.

I saw her in the hallway on Monday. When she saw me coming, she swiftly sliced through the crowd and disappeared. In science class, when I came in, the teacher abruptly stopped me at the door and told me the whole class was getting their science partners reassigned. I was paired up with a brutish boy by the name of Curtis. I took my seat next to him, in the very last row. When the lesson started, I looked around and realized that only four groups had switched partners.

Throughout the week, I felt like I was becoming Moses, and I was parting the Red Sea. When I'd walk through the hallways, groups would back away. I tried to reason that it was just my imagination, but it seemed more and more apparent that people were whispering about me as I walked by.

The following week, in passing, Candice said, "We had to take the kitten to the vet because he was really sick with worms, but he'll be okay. I love him so much."

That was the last time she ever spoke to me.

I kept my kitten, Odie, in my bedroom all the time. One day, for no particular reason, I took him upstairs. I was sitting at the kitchen table next to my brother. My mother was at the stove cooking.

Our white German Shepherd, Sugar, was eating out of her bowl. Odie came up behind Sugar and lifted his little paw to swipe my dog's tail. In a split second our dog had the kitten in her mouth. The dog whipped the kitten from side to side, then flung it sideways. The kitten's head slid under the china cabinet, and then its body seized, and we heard a loud snap, which was its little neck breaking.

I started screaming and stumbled outside onto the deck in shock.

My brother came out and said, "Get in the car, Mom said we're taking the kitten to the vet!"

I held my kitten's limp little body close to my heart as my mother sped down the road. We pulled into the vet's office and I sprinted in, holding my kitten out, crying hysterically.

I was sitting on a chair, sobbing, waiting with my brother. The vet came out and said, "I'm really sorry, he's already gone."

"Are you—"

"Let's go," my mother cut me off.

The vet handed her a white box.

I was in shock. It didn't occur to me what might be in the white box.

When we were back in the car and driving down the road, my mother said, "He didn't charge us."

That precious kitten had been my baby. Not only had I lost Candice, who was my only friend, but my baby Odie was gone now too. He had relied on me to keep him safe and I failed.

I felt so alone.

43

Lunch Money

It had been a three-day weekend, but school resumed Monday. My mother had been gone for a week and hadn't left any food or money in the house.

In the cafeteria, I looked down at my carton of chocolate milk, the lasagna oozing off the Styrofoam plate, the greasy breadstick, and the napkin and plastic fork, and my hands gripping the sides of the maroon plastic lunch tray. I was delirious from starvation and relieved to be in such close proximity to food.

"Thirty-seven," the lunch lady said, looking up agitated from the pile of pennies I had given her. She was sitting on a stool in front of the cash register.

I heard snickering behind me. "Um, okay," I said. I placed my lunch tray on the counter, and began patting my clothes. I knew I didn't have any more money. Reduced lunch cost forty-six cents.

"You're holding up the line," she impatiently huffed.

"Okay, sorry, one se—"

I was shoved forward and spun around.

"Move, you whore," a boy in my class said to me.

I stuttered as I took a step backward.

The boy and his friends stepped up as I tried to disappear into the background. Each boy placed his tray of food down, paid, then congregated at a table in the center of the room. I looked toward them. They were shoving each other and laughing.

"It's fine," the lunch lady said abruptly. "Just take your tray. But tomorrow you better have the forty-six cents."

I took my tray. I felt so unworthy of my lunch. I hung my head as I walked all the way to the back of the cafeteria. I sat alone in the far corner, looking into the sea of monsters eating around me. *Where am I going to get that forty-six cents?* I thought to myself. I ate every morsel of food on my tray and used my fork to scrape up every last bit of watery tomato sauce. That was the first thing I'd eaten that day, and I was pretty certain I wouldn't be having dinner.

Suddenly I was ripped out of my wave of self-pity. The double doors were kicked in, and a SWAT team came running in. The loud cafeteria immediately fell silent. The team rushed over to the table of boys that had been behind me in the lunch line. They yanked up two of the boys, led them to the wall, then instructed them to place their hands on the wall. Every single student in the lunchroom was silent and staring. It was so quiet that everyone could hear the low clink of the handcuffs tightening around their wrists. The boys were led toward the main office.

People immediately started clamoring. I just sat there in silence. I'd never seen anything like that. I had no idea what those two boys might have done. I could hear conversations from other tables, but it seemed like everyone was as clueless as me. Our high school wasn't really a dangerous place. There wasn't a lot of crime aside from idiots selling marijuana. *Maybe that's what it was*, I thought to myself. *They must have been selling drugs.*

The bell rang, and people began standing and putting their lunch trays away. I threw mine away, then looked over to the mostly abandoned table the boys had sat at. The trays of the two boys who had been arrested were still sitting on the table. I looked to my left and to my right. No one was watching me. I quickly hurried over to their trays and was able to snatch a half-eaten bag of Doritos, an apple, and two cartons of cranberry juice. I stuffed them into my backpack. I was so proud.

That was my dinner that night. I sat on my bed and grinned while I ate, wondering what had happened to the boys.

The next morning, I woke up for school. I came up the spiral staircase. My mother was sitting, staring with her mouth open, into the corner of the room. The television was on but was on mute.

"Mom," I said firmly.

"Huh?" she kind of made a noise. It wasn't really directed at me.

"Mom, I need lunch money." I was hopeful.

She didn't respond. I knew I'd be really hungry later that day. "Mom!" I said louder. I came all the way up the stairs, stood before her, at eye-level, and shouted, *"Mom*! I need lunch money *now!"*

She blinked slowly, sort of swayed back, and continued to stare into the corner of the room. I felt so much rage mounting inside me. I wanted to tear her apart. *Fucking forty-six cents!* was all I could think. Anxiety made me hold my breath. I clenched my fists and tensed my entire body. She was in another world.

I said, "I wish it was you who died, not Dad." I walked out the front door with no lunch money at all.

I don't remember how, but later I found out that those two boys had been arrested because, the weekend before, they filmed themselves at a house party raping a drunk girl with a banana, a cordless phone, and other household items.

44

I Know What I Saw

I woke up late at night to an unusually silent house. I strained in the darkness to hear remnants of domestic violence but heard nothing. I waited…Nothing. I had to pee. I got out of bed, cracked my door open, and strained to hear. Nothing. I crept to the spiral staircase, and again listened. Nothing. I stood on the first step, then the second. I skipped the third step because I knew it would make a loud squeak. I emerged from the basement and stood still in the living room, trying to hear Evan's distinctive snore. Nothing. I walked toward the bathroom. In the hallway I could see into my mother's bedroom. Her door was ajar. I saw her and someone else asleep in her king-sized bed. I watched for a moment as their chests rose and fell, but thought it was odd that neither of them were snoring.

I used the bathroom, headed back downstairs and went to sleep again.

In the morning I woke up early. It was Saturday, and Evan was usually there for breakfast. I listened, but I didn't hear his voice. I came upstairs to see my mother sitting at the kitchen table.

"Who slept over last night?" I asked nonchalantly.

"No one, why?" she responded.

I was confused. She always lied about a lot of things, but she wouldn't lie about having someone sleep over. In her mind, having a man sleep over was proof that she was still worth something, so it was often something she would gloat about.

"I don't care who it was," I said. "I was just wondering."

"Really, no one slept over," she said.

"I saw someone in your bed." I was adamant. "I came upstairs to go to the bathroom and I saw someone asleep in your bed."

"You're crazy, no one slept over." She got up from the kitchen table and moved toward her bedroom to make her bed. I watched her in disbelief from down the hall.

As she leaned over her bed, she realized my dad's half of the bed was, in fact, slept in. The sheets were all pulled up. My dad used to sleep with a pillow in between his legs. There was a pillow at the foot of the bed with an imprint in it, exactly the way my dad would have left it.

My mother came out of her room. She checked the front door. It was locked. She checked the back door. It was also locked. We looked at each other strangely.

"Maybe your father came to sleep with me?" Her voice was unusually meek.

"Maybe," I said, wanting to confirm her hopes.

"I haven't heard from your grandmother in a couple of days, and I just tried to call. She's not picking up the phone," she said. "Let's just go over there." She grabbed her purse and cellphone.

When we arrived at my grandmother's apartment complex, her car was in the parking lot. My mother used her extra key, and I followed her up the stairs.

"Vanna," my mother called.

There was no answer.

The living room was uncharacteristically messy with empty wine bottles, magazines, and clothes strewn about. There were empty pill bottles all over the coffee table.

"Vanna!" my mother called with more urgency as she went toward the kitchen.

I went to the bedroom. "Mom!" I shouted. My grandmother was lying face down on the floor, moaning and flexing her feet. I knelt down next to her and rolled her on her side. Her skin was clammy. White foam was oozing out of the corners of her mouth, and her naturally gray eyes were rolling back in her head.

My mother came in, cleared me away, knelt down next to my grandmother, and instructed me to call 9-1-1.

The ambulance came quickly. I watched as they strapped my grandmother onto a stretcher and maneuvered her down the steps of her second-story apartment.

I followed them downstairs and was surprised to see two girls from my class standing with a group of adults. I wasn't friends with the two girls.

"What happened?" one of them asked nosily.

I weighed my options, in terms of telling them. I didn't want to say that my grandmother was a suicidal, abusive alcoholic because I wanted to protect her privacy, but I also needed someone to talk to. I knew those girls weren't interested in being my friends.

"Kristy, let's go!" my mother called as she got into our purple minivan.

"My grandma is sick," I lied quickly as I hurried toward the car.

In the hospital my grandma had black straps across her chest, and her hands were fastened tightly to the rails of the hospital bed. She continued to moan, and rock her head side to side.

There was a catheter tube leading out from under the sheet she lay beneath.

My mother took me in the hallway. "Grandma's going to be okay," she assured me.

"The doctors induced vomiting and put the catheter in to get the drugs out of her. She's very sad about your father. She blames herself."

I thought back to the night my dad died, when he told us about his childhood. My grandmother had been a terrible parent. She let my dad starve and let strange men beat him, and she gave away his siblings. *Yeah, she should blame herself,* I thought. But then I thought about my mother and realized that all the things my grandmother had done and let happen to my dad, my mother was doing and letting happen to me.

This was the biggest revelation in my life. And from it, I knew I wanted my life to turn out better than my mother's, my dad's, and my grandmother's. I wanted to break the cycle and be happy.

45

It's Cold

Winter was the worst. Our house had no heat, except for a wood-burning stove. My mother spent all the money she had on drugs and her boyfriend, so she didn't get any wood. As September ended and October began, the house got progressively colder.

My bedroom was a storage room in the partially underground basement. There was no insulation or windows. The floor was concrete. There was a door to the garage and a heavy storm door to the driveway. A third door led to the rest of the house. In an effort to protect myself, I tried to always keep that third door locked.

To keep warm, I always lay in the fetal position. I would tuck my hands between my legs, bend them, and pull my knees close to my chest. I'd pile up as many quilts as I could find and create a barrier between my skin and the damp basement air. I'd pull the quilts up over my head and use my breath to warm the fortress I created beneath the blankets.

I didn't want to go to school anymore, because everyone hated me. I was starving and exhausted, and very, very tired of fighting. I decided to try to stay asleep as long as possible. For approximately a week I stayed under my blankets. I'd wake up occasionally to use the bathroom, then scurry back to my bed, lie down, and start my ritual of violently shaking my head back and forth to knock my brain around in my skull and make myself go back to sleep.

I groggily woke to Evan's dark frame bending over me. I tried to scream but he placed his hand over my mouth. *Fuck!* I thought. *The last time I went to the bathroom, I forgot to lock the door.* He slid his hand under the covers and between my legs. I flailed my arms and thrashed my head.

"Evan!" I heard my mother's drunk voice shout from upstairs. "Where the fuck are you?"

"Don't you dare talk to me like that, you stupid whore!" he shouted back to her.

With a firm and irritated thrust, he pushed me into the bed, stood up, snorted, and stomped out of my room. When I heard him ascend the stairs, I got up and locked my door.

I lay down, feeling very dirty and angry at myself for fucking up. If I hadn't forgotten to lock the door, that wouldn't have happened. It was my own stupid fault. I started crying heavily and felt like I deserved to be punished. I balled my hands into fists and began bashing myself in the head. I gave myself a couple of really solid blows. I wept and curled into the fetal position and cried for my dad until I eventually fell asleep.

The next morning, I heard each board of the spiral staircase bow under my mother's weight. I heard the reverberation of the mirrored doors of the basement closet as she drunkenly ping-ponged off of them. I heard the knock of her fist on the door, then I heard her slam all of her weight against the door, snapping it off its hinges. I heard her huff. I heard her grit her teeth. I heard her kick a cup over. I heard water spill onto the concrete and soak into the futon mattress. I heard her cock her open hand back, and I heard her connect with my temple. I heard the follicles rip from my scalp. I heard my skin scrape against the concrete. I heard the skin on my knees open, and I heard the blood spill out of the cuts. I heard my body drop onto the cold, hard floor. I heard the fibers of my lungs expand, and I heard the rage inside of my hallow gut.

And then I heard her lift her foot.

And then I heard her swiftly slam down.

And then I heard the snap.

And my eyes shot open.

And I heard myself let out a bloodcurdling howl.

And I heard her grab me by the back of the head.

And I heard her spit into my ear. I heard her say, "Get the fuck up and get to school."

And, I swear, I never felt a thing.

And then I heard her step over my body and stomp up the spiral steps.

I lay there on the concrete, in the fetal position, gripping my trap muscle, which was spasming from the trauma. I was sweating ice-cold sweat, and the vertigo kept me pinned to the concrete. I didn't feel any pain but knew something was very wrong. My right arm was completely numb and limp.

And then all of a sudden it was excruciating to breathe.

I knew she was going to come back down soon. I mustered everything in me to sit my weary, broken body upright. I looked down at my collarbone, which was protruding in an unnatural way. With my left hand I pulled a hoodie over my head and snaked my left arm into the sleeve. My right arm wouldn't move. I could hear her descending the staircase and staggered to my feet. Right as she entered the room, my vision became starry, and then everything went black.

She was dragging me by my hair down to the bus stop. I was struggling to force my feet to cooperate. She let go of my hair when I was twenty feet up the hill and shoved me in the direction of the bus stop. I prayed none of the kids saw her dragging me.

When I got down to where the streets intersected, I leaned against a stop sign to gain my composure. Finally, the pain began setting in. I gripped my arm, lifting it up and putting pressure on my shoulder. It was pulsing like a heartbeat.

In school I spent the entire day nursing my collarbone and shoulder. When I was alone in the bathroom, I gently lifted the hoodie up to inspect the damage. A large green-and-black bruise had formed over my collarbone and down my chest. I hoped I wasn't bleeding internally. I took shallow breaths and held my arm up, because I didn't know what else to do.

I never went to a doctor.

I don't remember exactly when, but around that time I stopped showering. It was too painful to wash my hair, and I got this idea in my head that maybe if I stopped showering, I would smell so bad that Evan wouldn't want to molest me anymore. It was an unreasonable decision, but I felt like I had very few options.

46

Hospital

My mother's drug habit was out of control. Every day was unpredictable. I never knew when or how long she'd be gone. She'd be away for a week at a time, leaving my brother and me without food or money. Other times, she'd be home on the living room couch, basically dead to the world.

Her bedroom door was locked, and I could hear she was on the phone.

"Mom," I knocked.

"Go the fuck away!" she shouted through the door.

"Mom, open the door. I need lunch money," I whined.

"If you don't go the fuck away, I'm going to beat you until you don't wake up," she threatened.

I rolled my eyes and went into the kitchen to look for something to eat for breakfast. I found some leftover pasta in the refrigerator, took it out, and put it in the microwave.

My mother's door opened, and she wearily made her way into the kitchen. "Aunt Beth is sick. She has cancer. I don't think she is going to make it through. Do you want to go to the hospital to see her?"

It must have been lung cancer. Her entire life, I'd begged her to give up smoking. She hadn't listened, so why should I care now?

"For what? To say 'I told you so?'" I callously shot toward her.

We went to the hospital. Aunt Beth was happy to see us. She'd always been a robust woman. In the hospital bed she looked deflated and weak, but she was still smiling. There was a tiny hissing sound from the oxygen tube in her nostrils. She was wearing a two-piece flannel button-down pajama set.

"Hi!" she said cheerfully.

"Hi, Aunt Beth," my brother and I said. Uneasily we gave her slight hugs. Seeing her so thin was extremely off putting.

She coughed, "Hold on." She reached her left arm across her body to get a cup of water from her bedside table. Her deflated breast fell out of the bottom of her top.

My eye's widened and I felt nauseous.

When she brought her arm back around, the fabric from her top covered her breast. I don't think she realized what had happened.

"How are you?" she asked me.

"I'm okay." Then feeling a sense of urgency to talk about anything to fill the awkward space in the room I went on. "I've been really busy at school with my technology project. The topic is manufacturing prototypes."

"That's great," my aunt said hopefully. "I always wanted to be a criminal investigator."

I was surprised. She had never really said anything like that to me. I almost forgot that she had ever been a child with hopes and dreams. To me, she seemed to stay the same age my entire life. She was a waitress in a diner for most of her adult life. For as long as I could remember, her hair had been gray. She'd always been the same weight. Until that point in the hospital, I had never noticed her being anything but how she'd always been.

A nurse came in the room and said, "I'm sorry to interrupt, but it's time to head down."

My aunt reached over to the table and picked up a cigarette. She held it in her fingers for a moment, then tucked it behind her ear. She said, "I haven't smoked one time since they put me in the hospital. I keep the cigarette with me all the time, but I haven't smoked it. I have to go down for chemo now. I love all of you."

That evening my mother made dinner, even though Evan wasn't there. It was really weird to sit at the table without him there. When my mother sat down, she told my brother and me about her mom, who had died when she was nine years old. She told us that after her mom died, her father took custody of her, but he had a lot of resentment toward her because he'd wanted a boy. She told us that she had mostly lived with her aunt, who never wanted children. She told us about the abuse she'd endured. She told us about Aunt Beth, who was eight years older than her, and that Aunt Beth was lucky she was a teenager and didn't have to live with their aunt. She said she felt really abandoned by her sister, whom she'd always looked up to. Then, she told us, things had gotten much better. She'd met our dad, and he was everything she'd ever hoped for. They knew when they were just children that they'd get married and live happily together. Toward the end of dinner, she took three pills. She said, "Your father is gone, and my sister is going to die soon. I don't have any family left. I'm completely alone." She stood up, went in her bedroom, and shut the door.

I thought to myself, *Am I not your family? I'm still here. Charley and Stefanie are still here. What did we do that was so wrong that makes you treat us so badly?*

A few days later Aunt Beth passed away. She didn't have a funeral or anything, like when my dad died. My mother's sorrow worsened. Every day she was drinking and doing drugs from the moment she woke up until she passed out somewhere.

Charley and I would come home and find her passed out on the front lawn. Other kids who got dropped off at our bus stop would walk by and stare.

"Help me," Charley would plead to me.

"No, fuck her," I would retort, feeling unbelievably embarrassed that our peers were looking on.

"Dad would have wanted you to help," Charley shot back.

With a huff, we'd hoist our mother up and sling her arms over our shoulders. The blinding pain from my broken collarbone was unbearable, but my brother was right. No matter what our mother did to us, she was the woman my dad loved, and I had to help.

47

That's How The Night Goes

My eyes opened. There was a loud thud above me.

It was pitch black in my basement bedroom. The weight of seven quilts pushed down on my naked body. I was surrounded by damp air from the concrete floor and improperly insulated walls. I rolled onto my back, sinking into the musty, old futon mattress which sat on the floor.

"You stupid fucking bitch!" Evan's voice roared down from the first floor overhead.

I lay there and thought about the words 'domestic dispute'. I thought about how it couldn't be a domestic dispute if the person causing the problem isn't domesticated. He was a beast, fueled by drugs and liquor, and I hated him.

My mother was screaming, and I thought, *What if she dies tonight?*

That wasn't the first time Evan beat her, and I was never sure if it would be the last. Throwing her across the house became normal, and the next day it would be like nothing had occurred at all. My stomach felt raw from starvation. The frigid moisture in the air burned the welts from when I'd been beaten with a belt a few nights ago. There was a constant dull ache from my collarbone injury.

My life would probably be better if she died, I thought.

I fell asleep.

I shifted and a tiny flash of light creeped through the barricade of quilts I spent my life under. The light sucked the air out of my lungs, and fear drenched me in frigid sweat. It startled me awake because it definitely was not supposed to be there. I was awake, but I was paralyzed. My eyes hurt, and I furrowed my brow as I adjusted to the light.

The quilts were ripped away, exposing my naked body.

What the fuck was that?

My body tensed, braced, and I went to scurry away.

He caught me by my hair and yanked me to the side.

Evan.

I struggled; I dug my nails into his hand, trying futilely to get him to release my hair.

He pushed all 250 pounds of his weight on my back. He was so heavy. He pushed all the air out of my body, smothering me. My head was buried in a pillow, but my limbs squirmed violently, trying to save myself from suffocation.

I realized that tonight wasn't going to be like other nights, where I would wake up to him groping me with one hand and masturbating with the other. On a normal night, I would wake up, and he'd be fondling my chest and trying to slip his hands between my legs. I'd push him away and he'd scurry out of the room and go back upstairs to continue doing drugs and watching porn with my mother.

But no. Tonight was not going to end like that at all.

The initial pain I felt was like being torn open from the inside.

It was like a thunderstorm. He thrusted, he grunted. He smacked, thrusted, moaned. He dug his nails into my skull. I fought the entire time. Every moan signified another jolt of agony, like lightning before thunder.

Daddy, come save me. Daddy, please come save me. I pleaded with the universe while I struggled for air.

I fought until everything went black. I gave in to the darkness. A wave of euphoric comfort washed over me and I slipped away.

When I woke up, I was in immense pain. Vertigo. I couldn't lift my head. The muscles in my abdomen were contracting. I thought, *Is this what hemorrhaging feels like?*

I was shivering.

I hadn't opened my eyes yet because I was so afraid to find out he would still be there, and I didn't want to see what he had done to me.

I lay for a long time on my side, eyes closed, shivering, insides pulsing. I felt moisture soaking the mattress.

I found the courage and lifted one eyelid a sliver. No one was there. I opened my eyes and tightened my abdomen to roll over. Severe pain shot from my vagina up to my gut, wrenching my heart. I howled and instinctively curled into the fetal position. My quilts were pushed against the wall. I mustered my courage and grabbed a couple quilts and pulled them over my body and head.

I lay for a long time in the darkness. I wanted to shift because whatever the moisture was that soaked my bed, it was stinging my skin. Every little movement was agonizing. The constant stinging ended up being a better option than one second of the pain caused by moving.

A wave of self-pity overtook me, and I began to sob. I softly called out, "Daddy, come save me. Daddy, why did you leave me?" I said it over and over. Through my tears and my pain, I begged the universe to bring him home to me, to protect me.

I fell asleep.

Because there were no windows, and because of how deeply I slept, and because I was so used to the feeling of starvation, time was an irrelevant concept. I had no idea how many hours or days I lay there like that.

I came into consciousness now and then, and every time I woke, I chose to drift back into my perpetual slumber, to remain as dead to the world as I felt inside my mind and soul.

My eyes opened. My heart started to race. I thought, *He's here again. Someone is in here.* Fear paralyzed me. I heard something crash and I tensed my entire body.

A hand gripped my hair.

"Get the fuck up and get to school." My mother was drunk.

I was still naked, still wet, still in more physical pain than I'd ever been in in my life.

I motioned that I was getting up. She released my hair and left the room. I stumbled and struggled and tripped over my feet. I could not put on underwear. I found a pair of my brother's black sweatpants. I looked down. Red blood was smeared across my legs. Some parts were crusted over. Some parts were wet. I moved my legs to put the sweatpants on and saw that my labia were extremely swollen.

I stood and waddled toward the downstairs bathroom, which was on the other side of the basement. I felt like I had to pee, so I squatted over the toilet, trying to keep my bloody legs from touching anything. I couldn't pee. It burned. I tried not to panic. I climbed onto the counter. I ran the water and used it to wash the blood off my legs. The cold water eased the pain of my swollen labia. I plugged the drain and let the sink fill up. I sank my bottom down into the cold water in the sink and let myself urinate. It burned, but it was bearable with the cold water diluting and numbing everything. I tried to look at my vagina in the mirror. I didn't recognize what I saw. I thought my organs must have been falling out of me.

I could hear my mother stumbling around upstairs. I was fearful that if she came back downstairs and saw that I wasn't dressed, she would beat me even more. I pulled myself out of the sink, patted myself dry, and pulled on my brother's dark, oversized sweatpants again. I found a sweatshirt that was covered in cat hair and pulled it over my head.

I started for the door that led to the driveway. I gripped my stomach. I felt like if I gripped harder, it would somehow ease the pain. I tried to force my legs together when I walked, in an attempt to appear more normal, but the pain made me trudge with my legs wide, on the blades of my feet. As I made my way down the hill, I knew other kids were gawking at me. I kept my head down. I hoped to disappear. I concentrated on trying to make the pain go away, and on gripping my stomach. I tried to stand tall. I tried to appear okay. I thought, *Who am I kidding?*

I stood off to the side, out of the way of the other kids. I was grateful because my brother was still in middle school, so he wasn't there to witness the disaster that was me. I started to think about how thirsty I was. My throat had cracks in it, like the sandy ground in the desert.

I heard the bus coming. I struggled to get where I knew it would stop. The brakes ground, making a loud screeching noise. All the kids climbed onto the bus. I was the last one. I looked up just long enough to see the bus driver looking down at me in disgust. I struggled to make it up the three steps, and before I got up the second, the bus started moving. I winced at the pain caused by the bus moving. The driver was obviously trying to focus more on her job than was required, because she didn't want to have to see me or deal with me or even say good morning. *In all honesty*, I thought, *she's not getting paid enough to deal with my shit.*

I smelled and I was a pitiful sight, and I knew that. I struggled up the stairs. I let my dirty, knotty hair hang in front of my face. It was a shield that protected me from the hateful glares of other students.

I took the first seat in the front of the bus. I realized I could not sit down. I bent my knee and sat on my heel, making it so my vagina didn't have to touch anything.

I noticed the blood had soaked into the sweatpants, causing them to stick to my legs. I was lucky I found a dark pair.

On the ride to school, I thought about what had happened. I thought about my brother, and that I was happy he didn't go to my school. I was happy he wouldn't be ridiculed for his filthy, crazy bitch of a sister.

The bus came to a stop in front of my school. I stayed where I was, anticipating that it would take a long time to get down those dreaded three steps. The cheerleaders filed down the aisle. Their chatter stopped as they passed me. When they'd gotten off the bus and were standing outside, I watched in my peripheral vision as they pointed and whispered about me. They laughed and turned and skipped into school.

More students filed past me. Some stared, most looked in the other direction. No one said anything directly to me.

I took a deep breath. *Okay, just three stairs*, I thought to myself. I came off my heel, extended my leg out, and shifted out of the seat. I dragged my other leg out. The bus driver cleared her throat. I heard bus brakes grinding. Another bus was arriving and the bus driver needed to pull away.

One step. Two steps. One more step. I clenched my teeth and jumped and blacked out for a moment. I was off the bus and on the pavement. Face down, palms and knees scraped. I looked past my shoulder and saw the other bus pulling up. I struggled to my knees and saw faces pressed up against the windows, staring at me, the dirty kid on the ground.

I pulled myself up and waddled.

Cliques walked past me.

Inch by inch, I made it to the doors.

Inside the school, I looked at the door to the bathroom. I looked at the people filtering in and out. I didn't want to be in the bathroom with those people.

People furtively glanced at me and turned away. I was the topic of their morning. I saw a girl down the hallway opening a wrapper to a blueberry muffin from the cafeteria. From fifteen feet away, I swear I could smell the muffin. I watched as her boyfriend came up behind her and smacked her butt. She spun around, giggled, and threw her arms around his shoulders.

My stomach grumbled but then I realized the blood was soaking into the pants more. I had to do something quickly, otherwise I'd start leaving behind a crimson trail. I dragged myself into the bathroom.

Luckily, I found an open stall. I slipped off my flip-flops and leaned against the stall. I slid my sweatpants off. There was more blood covering my legs than there had been when I woke up. Bending over caused immense pain, but I knew I had to do something about the blood. I reached down and unrolled toilet paper. I pushed off the stall and bent over to wipe my legs. I looked back and realized I had smeared blood on the wall. *Stupid me. I'm going to get in so much trouble.* I dropped the blood-soaked toilet paper into the toilet and unrolled more. I sat on the toilet while I cleaned the wall. My wiping wasn't do anything except smearing the blood around more. *God, I'm so fucking stupid!*

I sat on the toilet, held my stomach, and nervously shook my legs. I tried to concentrate on the other people in the bathroom. I felt like if I concentrated hard enough, I could somehow will them to leave. One by one they exited. The bell rang and everyone went to class.

I reached over and pulled my slimy, sticky sweatpants back on and wiggled my feet into my flip-flops.

With tremendous effort, I stood. I looked down at the toilet. It was a disgusting mess of toilet paper and blood. I plodded to the door, cracked it open, and stuck my head out. I saw the school's police officer down the hallway. I pulled my head back inside and quickly scurried back into the stall. I didn't want to get in trouble for being late to class. I pulled my pants back down, sat on the toilet, and rested my head against the cool metal of the stall. I realized I had a fever. I gripped my pulsating stomach and fell asleep.

The bell rang and startled me awake.

I unrolled more toilet paper and dabbed at my vagina. It burned and I couldn't wipe, so I just dabbed. *Okay, good enough.* I pulled my pants up. Much of the blood had dried and now was crusty and flakey.

I slogged into the crowded hallway. *What period is it?* I had no idea. I saw the school's police officer walking toward me. I turned to get away from him. I heard him call my name, but I disappeared into the crowd and left him behind. *Where should I go?*

In the middle of the year, I had chosen not to take lunch, because everyone hated me, and I never had the forty-six cents for reduced lunch anyway. I also got a doctor's note because of my broken collarbone, so I didn't have to take gym class. I replaced lunch and gym with technology, which was also my two electives. So, out of nine periods, four were spent with my technology teacher, who was the only teacher I liked. That meant that more than likely, I should be in technology.

In the classroom, my technology teacher, Mr. Butler, stood against the SmartBoard. I adored him. My wonderful, colorblind, twenty-three-year-old teacher with orange hair and blue eyes and his purple button-down shirt and green slacks.

"Kristen," he said, surprised to see me. "Where are you supposed to be this period?"

Damn it, I thought to myself, *it's not tech time.* I stood there. I didn't say anything. He approached me. He was one of the only people in the world I didn't hate.

"Are you okay?" he asked me in a concerned voice.

I nodded.

"Are you sick?" he pressed.

"I don't know," I responded.

He looked at me, not through me, not past me, and not because I smelled or looked disgusting. He didn't look at me because he wanted to molest me or hit me or yell at me. He looked at me because he cared about his students. He cared and made me believe that I could earn an education, that I could become a professional, and be worth something, and be normal, and some day have a normal life.

Students started entering the classroom. "Kristen, you have to go to class," he said firmly. "Here, I'll write you a late pass. Where do you have to go?"

I asked, "What period is it?"

"Why don't you know what period it is?" he responded.

I stared into his eyes. I looked down at his pen and the green pad of late passes. I took a deep breath.

"It's sixth period," he said.

"Biology," I said.

He scribbled and tore off a late pass. I bowed my head and turned to leave. I schlepped into the hallway.

"Kristen," he called after me. I stopped and looked back at him. He pointed to the linoleum and there was a single drop of blood on the floor. "Mr. Malta, come watch my class," he called to another teacher. "Kristen, are you bleeding?" he asked. His face went pale. He motioned his hand and I followed him across the hall into his office. He sat at his desk and I squatted on the heel of my foot again.

I was scared. I feared I was going to get in trouble for the bloody mess I had left in the bathroom. My mother was going to beat me for missing class. The vice principal was going to yell at me, and tell me I was stupid, and I really hated her. But I knew I needed help. The bleeding and the pain weren't going away.

"My mom..." I started to speak. I was terrified. I hadn't even admitted to myself what happened yet. "... My mom's boyfriend..." I paused. Mr. Butler's eyes widened and he sucked in his breath. I stopped and felt a lump growing in my throat.

Mr. Butler turned and reached for his lunchbox. My mouth began to salivate. He opened it and gave me what was inside: a bottle of orange juice, a tuna-fish sandwich, a bag of Doritos, and a banana. He said, "I'll be right back. Stay here." He got up and left the room.

For a couple of minutes I forgot about all the pain and exhaustion. I enjoyed the meal my teacher had given me. I felt like a dog because I was so happy to see food.

When he returned, he was followed by the school nurse. I still hated her for the cheerleading incident, so I felt betrayed when I saw her. She smiled but I didn't smile back. I felt ambushed.

"How are you feeling?" she asked.

I didn't respond.

"Can you walk?"

I nodded.

"Okay," she sighed. "Come with me." I sensed she was annoyed that she had to deal with me. I begrudgingly followed her to the nurse's office. I was glad Mr. Butler came with us. Another student was lying down. The nurse said, "Okay, Michelle, time to head back to class." The other student whined momentarily, then compliantly accepted a hall pass, looked me up and down, and left the room. The nurse motioned for me to lie down. I didn't move. She reached over on her desk and retrieved a cookie. I felt defeated. I obeyed food. I admired food. I could smell the cookie from across the room. Like a dog who would lie down for a treat, I knew I would lie down for the cookie. *I am a dog.*

I looked at the cot and thought about the practicality of lying down. I knew it was going to hurt. I picked up one knee and tried to slide my other leg onto the cot. I gripped my stomach with one hand, and gently tried to ease myself down.

"Come on," the nurse said harshly. "I don't have time for games—"

Mr. Butler cut in with a stern voice I'd never heard him use, "She's not playing a game."

I was lying on the cot and felt a tiny smile in my heart. The smile didn't make it to my face, but I think he knew I was grateful that he'd stood up for me. I watched the nurse. She looked at my teacher, put the cookie down, and picked up her thermometer. I felt tricked. I was supposed to get the cookie. That was just one more reason to hate her. She came over and put the thermometer under my tongue. A few seconds later, it beeped, and she looked down. She shook her head in disapproval. She put her wrist on my forehead, then petted my hair. *I am a dog.*

She stood, turned, and tried to block my view. She wiped her hand on her pant leg, trying to get the grease from my hair off her manicured fingers and polished skin. She muttered something quietly to my teacher, then left the room. I looked into Mr. Butler's eyes. He was fifteen feet away. He looked over at the desk, snatched the cookie, and gave it to me. He retreated to the other side of the room and stared out the window. He was acting really weird, which I didn't understand.

I fell asleep.

I woke up and the school's guidance counselor was standing over me. I also hated her for kicking me out of the 'dead-parents club'. "Kristen?" she called. I looked over her shoulder. The principal, both vice principals, and the nurse were looking at me with blank expressions. I realized Mr. Butler was gone.

"Kristen, you're going to the hospital. We called for an ambulance. You're going to be okay."

I moaned in disapproval.

"You have a 103 fever, you're bleeding. You need to see a doctor immediately."

Fine, I thought to myself, *I don't care.* I was just so tired.

EMTs arrived and sat me in a wheelchair. I sat on my side because my vagina was still hurting so badly. I looked back at the cot. There was blood smeared on the lower portion of it. We passed by open classroom doors and my peers pointed and were whispering.

The EMTs helped me up and laid me on a cot outside. There was a lot of clanking as they wheeled me into the ambulance. When the ambulance started rolling, the cot started bouncing. I thought back to a technology project my friend, Sarah, had designed. She was a volunteer EMT and had created a device that could be strapped to a cot to stabilize a patient's broken arm during the drive. I realized, as my broken body was jostling around, that her invention was a really great idea. I fell asleep.

I woke up hazy and disoriented. I realized I was in the hospital. My legs were in stirrups and I was shivering under the thinnest blanket in the world. I lifted my head slightly to see a doctor between my legs. At least twelve other people, all wearing white coats were gathered behind the doctor, staring at my vagina. I look to my left and there was an older woman with a clipboard. I looked to my right and there was a female police officer and a couple other women who I didn't recognize.

I started to panic.

I started to hyperventilate.

Suddenly I shrunk to the size of a mouse. The doctor's torsos elongated and they were sixteen feet tall, peering down at me. My perception was completely distorted, fish-eyed, and I tried to kick away. I flailed my arms and started to scream. I needed to get away.

I felt hands hold my ankles down.

Two women rushed to my side. One held me down, the other shushed me and told me everything was going to be okay. I thrashed my head side to side and felt something tightening around my ankles. I felt something warm traveling up my arm, and a moment later I fell asleep.

I woke up in a new room. The same woman holding the clipboard from earlier was sitting next to my bed. The ridiculously thin white blanket was still draped over my body. The woman rose and stood over me.

"Kristen," she started. "Do you know who I am?"

I said nothing.

"I'm with the state's child protective services. I'm here to help you. My name is Kathy. How are you feeling?"

"I—I'm just really tired," I responded, unsure of what she meant by helping me.

"That's perfectly understandable, dear," she softly told me. "You've been through a lot. Rest as long as you need to, and when you're ready, we'll talk about what will happen next."

I fell back asleep.

"Kristen." Two doctors in white coats stood at the foot of my bed. A nurse stood to my right. I noticed an IV in my arm.

The nurse spoke, asking me permission, "I'm going to take your temperature, okay?"

I opened my mouth for the thermometer.

The social worker moved the chair to the other side of the room and was busily scribbling on her clipboard.

The thermometer beeped. The nurse took it out and looked at it. "100," she said. The doctors nodded their heads.

One of the doctors looked through me, coldly, and he said, "Kristen, we believe you've contracted genital herpes."

I let out a soul-wrenching howl. Tears streamed down my face. I cried and choked on my tears and mucus. I was being stoned to death. My first thought was of becoming a mother. I thought about how no one would ever want me, how I would never be able to have healthy babies.

The social worker stood, came to my side, and rested her hand on my shoulder. I lifted my arms and pressed my hands to my face.

"It's okay, I'm here for you." The social worker said.

I cried so loudly that I could barely hear her. I didn't care if I woke the entire hospital.

"I can answer any questions you may have," the second doctor said in a much more sympathetic tone than the first doctor had.

Then the first doctor left the room.

I continued to cry hysterically.

"You will still be able to have babies. There's medication we can give you to minimize the outbreaks. You won't die from this, and the worst is over." The doctor was trying to educate me over my howling.

Nothing anyone could say would make me feel better. My life was ruined. I was destroyed. I felt lower than I had ever felt. I felt like a worthless piece of shit.

Eventually, I calmed down. There were still tears, but my howling subsided. I managed to choke out, "When I have children, will they get it?"

"No, as long as you have a C-section, they won't get it," the doctor assured me.

We went back and forth, and she answered more of my questions. She told me I would have to be in the hospital for a week or two. She told me they had performed emergency surgery. She said my urethra had been torn. She told me there were stitches, which would dissolve inside me, and that I had a catheter. I had sores and I should expect them to burst, and that when they did it would hurt very much, but they'd continue to give me pain medicine to help. She told me they were monitoring my fever and working to get it down.

The next day the nurse came back in.

"I have to change your IV or it will get infected."

I began to cry.

"You know you hit me the first time I put it in." She turned so I could see the black-and-blue mark on the other side of her face.

I cried.

"It's okay, though," she said. "I can imagine you were very scared."

I didn't recall hitting her. I didn't remember the needle at all.

"Would you like to take a shower?"

I nodded.

The nurse helped me up. I had to hold the catheter as I traipsed. The shower was across the hall, about fifteen feet away.

I began to cry when I saw how far away it was. It seemed like an endless distance.

"It's okay, you can do it," the nurse said sweetly.

I waddled and was grateful that no one except the sweet nurse was there to witness that painful journey.

In the shower there was a hook to hang the catheter. It was disgusting to look at. My fever made me feel nauseous and light-headed. I hung the catheter and realized that, like a dog, I was leashed to the wall.

As the water trickled down my body, it burned my vagina. I tried to stand so the water wouldn't run onto it. The IV in my arm hurt, and I couldn't bend it, so I used my free hand to wash my hair and my body.

Suddenly the steam was too much, the ground too wet. My eyes rolled back, and I thought I sat down. I woke up to two nurses pulling me from the steamy shower, onto the cold tile floor. I'd fallen unconscious.

I woke up in my bed in unthinkable agony. I rang the red call button. The nurse came in and told me I had passed out. She said that when I did, the catheter ripped out of me and tore open some of the stitches, so the doctors had restitched. She told me that later I would have to have an MRI to make sure I was okay from the fall.

I fell asleep.

I woke up to darkness. It was the middle of the night. My fever was so high. I thought I was dying. I rang the red call button. I needed help. I was in a lot of trouble.

I rolled over. I tried to stand. I blacked out and reached out for a tray to try to stabilize my wobbly legs. As I fell to the ground, the tray crashed, the clatter deafening.

I woke to nurses buzzing around me, and I was hoisted onto a rolling bed. A man pushing the bed wheeled me down to the elevator, down another hall, through double doors, and into a room. He told me he was going to move me into the MRI machine. He briefly explained that I would have to lie still, and there would be loud noises. It would seem like I was in there for a long time.

I lay in the machine, looking up, trying to keep my head still. There were loud knocking sounds and buzzing noises, and I realized I had an atrocious headache. I lay still and thought about my mother. *Will she come visit me? Does she care that I am in the hospital?* I wanted to know where she was, what she was doing, and if she was thinking about me.

Finally, the MRI was over. I was removed from the machine and wheeled back up to my room. I settled back into my bed when two nurses came in.

"We have to change your catheter."

Before I had a second to react, the larger nurse was holding me down. I started to scream and kick. The other nurse ripped out the catheter, sending shooting pain through my abdomen. I howled and flailed. *This better be over*, I thought to myself. The larger nurse didn't let go. I hollered at the top of my lungs.

A second blow.

She jammed another catheter inside of me.

I howled.

I am a fucking dog.

They left the room and I cried and cursed, and I was alone.

Alone. Alone. Alone. I am alone.

I thought about my dad. The very last thing he said to me, the night he died was, "The only thing everyone in the world has in common is that they feel alone."

He killed himself, and finally, lying alone in that hospital bed, I understood why.

Epilogue

I always thought I was this piece of shit that lived in the basement. I believed I was the only one who was hated, and I was the only one who was molested. I was the only one who wasn't loved. What happened to me was something ridiculous.

After the hospital I was sent to live in foster care. My brother briefly came with me, but it was quickly determined that he was not in imminent danger, and the state decided to send him back to live with my mother.

My mother was ordered to take parenting classes and drug rehab. Neither helped her. She's still alive, though still an extremely unhealthy, depressed, alcoholic drug addict.

My mother's boyfriend was arrested, tried, and sent to prison. Because of a legal technicality he served under two years. His wife never left him. Two of his children died of drug overdoses. I don't know what happened to the third.

All of the girls who started the rumors about me grew up to be losers. The one who was the source of most of the rumors grew up to have three children by three different men who all abandoned their kids. She ended up committing an armed robbery and went to prison for four years. Carissa, Lily, and Lindsay all had similar outcomes.

Alyse grew up to be a clinical psychologist, and our friendship lasted into our adult lives (though it disintegrated some time ago). Despite the current condition of our relationship, she is a wonderful person and I wish her all the best in this world.

When I was nineteen years old, I was diagnosed with narcolepsy with cataplexy. Narcolepsy is a neurological sleep disorder characterized by excessive daytime sleepiness, an inability to control my circadian rhythm, and a malfunction in my brain, which can't pull itself out of REM sleep. Cataplexy is a sudden loss of muscle control. Sometimes I feel like the universe granted me narcolepsy so I could survive that turbulent time in my childhood. When I was diagnosed, it explained a lot about my life, and how I was able to sleep through so much of my abuse.

In my next book, I'm going to write about what else happened. I'm going to write about my escape. I'm going to write about how I got help, and about a kindness in human beings that I didn't know existed when I was starving in the darkness.

Thank you for reading my book. You made me feel less alone.

About the Author

The author, Christy Monroe, is a stripper and nationally touring headlining comedian. She lives in Brooklyn, NY with her two dogs and cat. This is the first book she's written. Please visit her website at www.strippercomedy.com.

Additional Resources

National Suicide Prevention Lifeline
1-800-273-8255
www.suicidepreventionlifeline.org

National Human Trafficking Hotline
1-888-373-7888
SMS 233733 (Text "HELP" or "INFO")
www.humantraffickinghotline.org

National Center for Missing and Exploited Children
www.missingkids.org

National Sexual Assault Telephone Hotline
1-800-656-4673
www.rainn.org

An online community for strippers:
www.wearedancersnyc.com

Harm reduction, political advocacy, and health services for sex workers:
www.desireealliance.org

National Eating Disorder Helpline:
1-800-931-2237
www.nationaleatingdisorders.org

Domestic Violence Prevention Society:
1-866-237-5888
www.sagesse.org

Author's Note

If you are being abused, please hear me when I say it, you do not deserve to be mistreated. There is no amount of time that passed, or damage that has been done that makes you unworthy of respect, medical help, mental health help, and love. Reach out. You might be shocked, like I was, to find out that even strangers can show incredible kindness. The truth is, they might not. The truth is, you might not get the help you need from judges, police officers, doctors, or teachers. But keep reaching out. You are valuable, beautiful, and I love you.

When I was an adult, many, many years later, a boy from my school reached out to me on Facebook. This was many years before I wrote this book. He said he was sorry he didn't help me back then. I responded, "it's okay. You would have had no way of knowing what I was going through." His response shook me to the core. He said, "that's the thing. I did know. Everyone knew. Parents and teachers knew. At football games in the bleachers parents would be standing around talking about you. We knew, and we didn't take action, and I am sorry."

If you know, or think you know that someone is being abused, especially a child, please do something to stop it. Abused people have an incredible ability to reason why they are being abused. They can't always ask for help. They can't always speak against their abuser. This does not mean they don't need help. Even if you don't want to get directly involved, you can always leave an anonymous inquiry with your local police department. Five minutes of your time could save someone's life.

If you are an abuser, get help. Facing the consequences of your actions, no matter how severe, will ultimately free you. Not Evan, but someone else I know was an abuser, and that person was caught. That person ultimately went to prison for a long time. I know, in intimate detail, that despite the fact that prison is a nightmare, that person knows that getting caught saved them, and saved other people who would have been victimized by them. Admitting fault is one of the most selfless acts, and by admitting fault, I genuinely believe God will forgive you.

Made in United States
North Haven, CT
11 April 2024